shape their lives, their professions, and their societies.

Grand Valley Celebrates 50 Years of Shaping Lives

ISBN: 978-1-61623-896-490000

Published by Grand Valley State University.

Printed by Custom Printers in Grand Rapids, Michigan, United States of America.

Printed on paper manufactured with electricity in the form of renewable energy (wind, hydro, and biogas), and includes a minimum of 10% postconsumer recovered fiber. Trees used to manufacture this paper are certified from sustainably managed forests.

Sara,

I'm so glad you were on the LVR staff. It's been a pleasure getting to know you. Have a great summer and good luck next year!

— Maizie

Breezy! You are so fun! It was awesome being on staff with you this year :)

♡ Marellia

We are going to have so much fun this summer! I have really enjoyed working with you this year and I'm going to miss you on staff next year!

♡ Kylie Laudenslager

Breezy,

It's been great working on staff with you and getting to know you better!

Best of luck with your future endeavors!

— Sean Pollard

I had a great time getting to know you and working with you! — Tyler

I'm so glad I got to meet you! Thanks for the wonderful past couple of months and welcoming me in!

You're the best!

~ Andrew

Sara/Breezy!

I have been so happy and appreciative of your work and smile this year. I can't wait to see what the future has in store for you.

Ashley

Fall 2007

Circa 1972

TABLE OF CONTENTS

CONTENTS

APPENDIX

Pictured are Grand Valley presidents in the Richard M. DeVos Center, 2009. From left are Arend D. Lubbers, Mark A. Murray and Thomas J. Haas. James H. Zumberge (1923-1992) served as the university's first president.

FOREWORDS BY THREE PRESIDENTS

In its first 50 years Grand Valley has emerged as one of the nation's most successful regional universities. Many years ago I was asked what programs we emphasized. I replied that our vision was an institution of high quality in all areas, not one that favored a few. That, I believe, has happened. The excellence of instruction and the efficiency of management distinguish the university and provide the foundation for continuing achievements in the next half-century.

– AREND D. LUBBERS, PRESIDENT 1969-2001

This book portrays great accomplishments of the past 50 years. I hope it also prompts our commitment to the next 50! Our first 50 years were a compelling tale of building a community that helps students form and achieve worthy aspirations while approaching the day's challenges with the timeless wisdom that derives from a liberal education. Let's make the next 50 years the same. As Ernie Banks says – "Let's play two!"

– MARK A. MURRAY, PRESIDENT 2001-2006

What a privilege it is to be leading this university community as it marks its 50th anniversary. The three presidents who came before me have worked creatively and diligently to leave Grand Valley ever stronger. I am grateful to them and to the wonderful faculty and staff members who have built this university.

This celebratory book is a look back at our history, a history that builds our expectations of this fine university's place in the future. Grand Valley is meeting the challenge of teaching students who will lead in the 21st century. My unbridled optimism and firm expectation has always been that the best of Grand Valley State University is yet to come.

– THOMAS J. HAAS, PRESIDENT 2006-

L. William Seidman, 1961

A STORY BUILT ONE BRICK AT A TIME

1

IF EVERYTHING STARTS AS AN IDEA, whose idea was it to start what is now Grand Valley State University? The credit for the big idea, the creative energy and the political acumen goes to the late L. William Seidman. The Grand Rapids native received an undergraduate degree from Dartmouth College, manned a destroyer during World War II and earned a law degree from Harvard University and an MBA from the University of Michigan. He worked for three U.S. presidents and chaired the Federal Deposit Insurance Corporation from 1985 to 1991. These are highlights from a tremendous career of a man who remained active until his death in 2009 at the age of 88.

But before his days on the national scene, this "plain talking accountant," as the *New York Times* called him in 2009, had a mission in West Michigan.

Seidman had read a legislative report in the late 1950s that stated young people in West Michigan were going to college at a lower rate than elsewhere in the state. The Russell Report concluded that a new four-year college in the Grand Rapids area was needed. Seidman set about to fill the need, but he had to get the community behind the idea to make it reality.

Seidman began marshaling support for a West Michigan college at a lunch he arranged at the Pantlind Hotel, now the Amway Grand Hotel, in downtown Grand Rapids. He invited a small group of influential community leaders, including Robert H. Bennett Jr., Martin Buth, David E. Dutcher, James Idema, Harry Lawford, F. William McKee, Richard VanderVeen, Robert Van Ess and Robert G. Watkins.

Seidman said he told the group: "You know I think this city is one of the most wonderful cities that I have been in, and I have been in quite a few, but it really lacks something, and that is public higher education. I think we all ought to get together and see if we can bring it to Grand Rapids."

The pivotal group confirmed that indeed Seidman had a good idea.

He also had high hopes.

Aerial view of downtown Grand Rapids, upper Monroe Avenue, 1957.

Pictured is Campau Square with the Pantlind Hotel on the left.

Congressman Gerald R. Ford, circa 1950.

Richard Gillett and Seidman, center, were among the early supporters of establishing a college in West Michigan.

As the citizens committee grew and traveled all over the region and met with every community organization that would have them, committee members would set up a tape recorder, and Frank Sinatra's "High Hopes" would ring through the room. It became the theme song for the campaign to bring a public higher education institution to the area.

"You know the song 'High Hopes,' the ant moving the rubber tree plant? We did that for about a year," Seidman said. "I must have gone to hundreds of meetings. We would entertain people at our house usually a couple of times a week."

Seidman said there was great support from the community. Eventually the Committee for the Establishment of a Four-Year College included a long list of influential leaders, such as then Congressman Gerald R. Ford, Edward H. Frey, former Congressman Richard VanderVeen, Francis C. Campau, Duncan E. Littlefair and William L. Sherwood. In 18 months the committee was ready to pitch its idea to the Legislature and Governor G. Mennen Williams in Lansing.

Legislative support came, but with a hefty assignment – raise $1 million and get a university charter.

As Seidman later described it, they began raising money for a promise. Key players were area banks – specifically Old Kent Bank and its president Richard (Dick) Gillett – companies and labor unions. Individual citizens got involved, paying $1 for a brick; brick by brick they raised $1 million and built a university.

Members of the first Board of Control are pictured; left to right, back row, Edward J. Frey, James Copeland, Dale Stafford, William Kirkpatrick, Icie Macy Hoobler, Kenneth Robinson; left to right, front row, Arnold Ott, Grace Kistler and L. William Seidman.

Williams signed the bill that established Grand Valley State College as Michigan's 10th state-supported, four-year college on April 26, 1960. The bill also provided for the governor to appoint a Board of Control. Williams appointed Seidman; Frey, president of Union Bank and the Grand Rapids Chamber of Commerce; Grace Kistler, former president of the Michigan Federation of Women's Clubs; Dr. Arnold Ott, president of Ott Chemical Company; Dale Stafford, editor and publisher of the *Greenville Daily News*; Kenneth Robinson, director of Region 1-D, AFL-CIO; James Copeland, president of Security National Bank and Wyoming State Bank; Dr. Icie Macy Hoobler, biochemist from Ann Arbor; and William Kirkpatrick, president of Kalamazoo Paper Box Company. The minutes from the board's first meeting, held in Williams' office in October 1960, stated that Seidman was elected chairman by a "unanimous and enthusiastic" vote.

Shortly before he died in May 2009, Seidman said: "I've had a great life. I've worked for three presidents of the United States. I've been in major business and involved in other educational endeavors. There's nothing that I've done in life that gives me the satisfaction of seeing how Grand Valley State University is delivering on its promise to the western Michigan area."

– BY MARY EILLEEN LYON

COMMITTEE FOR THE ESTABLISHMENT OF A FOUR-YEAR COLLEGE

NOVEMBER 22, 1958

Willis I. Anderson
Ralph B. Baldwin
Gerald Barnes
Richard B. Baxter
Stanley B. Benford
Dr. Howard G. Benjamin
Julius Bergama
Melville R. Bissell, III
Allen Boelens
William H. Bouwkamp
Arthur N. Branson
Frank K. Bray
Philip W. Buchen
Benjamin J. Bulkema
Dr. Robert I. Byram
Francis C. Campau
Rev. Donald V. Carey
Clark C. Caskey
Lynn H. Clark
Dr. Griffith S. Cossar
Thomas Crawford
Ben D'Orazio
James R. Danenberg
Herbert G. Daverman
Ben Dean
Bill DeMar
Richard J. DeVries
F. William Dunn
Minor D. Dutcher
Irene T. Eberhard
E.J. Erickson
Rabbi Harry Essrig
Congressman Gerald R. Ford
Norman Freeman
Edward J. Frey
Richard M. Gillett
Paul G. Goebel
Clyde I. Green, DC
H. Samuel Greenswall, Sr.
Chester A. Hall
David E. Hanson
Mary Houran
Dr. Raymond E. Huldin
Mary Ann Janowiak
Earl M. Johnson
Mrs. Siegel W. Judd
Harry J. Kelley
Charles M. Kindel
Frank Klackle
John A. Kloosterman
Donald W. Kohlstedt
Carol F. Kuhlmann
Vaner E. Laine
Henry T. Lathrop
Charles LeBaron
Lee Libby
Dr. Duncan E. Littlefair
Phyllis MacKay
Mrs. James Malecki
Harry D. Marshall
Rev. Joseph Q. Mayne
Zillah M. Meeker
Mrs. George Meyer
Wendell A. Miles
Morris B. Morningstar
John G. Mothoek
Mrs. Carl A. Nelson
Mrs. John Parks
Edwin Parmeter
Mrs. Florence Peterson
Harley Peterson, Jr.
Leland D. Phelps
Larry Pierce
DeForest Poole
Ralph H. Pratt
Dr. Jay L. Pyleman
C. Fenton Raber
Wilbur Reister
Mrs. Hollis E. Reynolds
Robert W. Richardson
James W. Riordan
Kenneth W. Robinson
Ernest W. Ruehs
Elisabeth Sage
Richard F. Scanlon
William J. Schulling
Walter C. Schultze
William L. Sherwood
Arthur Silverstein
Franklin G. Sisson
Elton R. Smith
Forrest Squires
Robert K. Stolz
Alexander H. Stuart
M.R. Sturr
Samuel W. Tamminga
Miriam O. Tillman
Robert S. Tubbs
Eleanor Turnath
Lyle E. VanDenBerge, II
Richard F. VanderVeen
Joseph VanDyk, Jr.
J.E. Vaneklasen
Marion J. Viall
Dr. John E. Visser
Victor H. Weller
Rev. James W. Wright

Teri L. Losey
Secretary

LEADERS

2

"IF YOU BUILD IT, [THEY] WILL COME." That famous line from the Kevin Costner film "Field of Dreams" seems more than appropriate for Grand Valley.

Remember the cornfield in the movie? The cornfield in Allendale was set aside not only for a baseball diamond and a football stadium but also first and foremost for a thriving university.

At its 50th anniversary Grand Valley is the academic home to more than 24,000 students. A string of gifted leaders and generous supporters created and guided Grand Valley State from a college, to colleges and finally to the university it is today.

The legislation that established Grand Valley required the founders to provide a campus. Richard (Dick) Gillett, then head of Old Kent Bank, spearheaded the effort to acquire land. A committee was formed to decide where in the region to locate the campus. Sites were proposed for the Muskegon area; arguments were made for locating close to Holland or closer to downtown Grand Rapids. The group proposing the Allendale location had an option on the land, and it was deemed centrally located and close enough to Grand Rapids that people could commute. Arnold Ott, Board of Control member, said that after flying over the Allendale site he felt the "beauty of it could not be bought for a million dollars."

From left, L. William Seidman, Governor John Swainson and James H. Zumberge hold a detonator at the groundbreaking ceremony, 1962.

Vice President of Business Affairs Philip W. Buchen, left, and Sen. Frank D. Beadle stand by the sign in front of the university's Office of Administration at the Grey House, 1962.

Governor John B. Swainson speaks at the groundbreaking ceremony. Zumberge and Seidman join him on the platform, August 1962.

Members of Michigan's House and Senate hold a provisional Grand Valley College seal, circa 1960.

There was a contest to come up with the name, and a citizens committee eventually settled on Grand Valley State College.

"The first thing it took was to get somebody to work for this new entity," said founder L. William Seidman. "Since I was the chairman of this new organization, I went out to hire a president and to get some faculty in place."

Work began in earnest. The board named Philip Buchen as the first officer of Grand Valley State College. Buchen was the law partner of then Congressman Gerald R. Ford, and he had been serving as volunteer counsel for the board. Board members Seidman, Grace Kistler and Ott were appointed to the search committee to find the president.

In February 1962, the Board of Control hired James H. Zumberge, a renowned geologist from the University of Michigan, to be the first president. The board also hired the first faculty members and in August 1962 broke ground on Lake Michigan Hall. Fifteen pioneer professors became the faculty for the College of Arts and Sciences.

"We told the faculty, 'You go out and recruit the students, and if you don't come back with students, just keep going because there isn't going to be any school here,'" Seidman remembered. The new faculty members were armed with promotional brochures, which read in part: "The college will be searching for able surprises – students with a talent for creativity who give promise of rising to the challenge of an imaginative college program."

Buchen reviews the Allendale Campus map, 1963.

Zumberge, a noted geologist and Grand Valley's first president, is shown at the site of a highway overpass in Grand Rapids, circa 1964.

Architect William Kessler shows Zumberge the model of the interior of Lake Michigan Hall, 1962.

Zumberge took the reins of this new college from 1962 to 1968. In his book, *Grand Valley State College: Its Development Years 1964-1968*, Zumberge wrote: "I have had the unusual experience of seeing a cornfield transformed into a vigorous young college. I would be less than honest if I did not admit to frequent periods of despair during these years; others with me experienced similar feelings. We did not succumb, however, because within all of us there was a fierce determination to make Grand Valley what the founders wanted it to be."

In 1963, 226 students enrolled in Grand Valley State College. In his look back, Zumberge cited pride in the physical campus, the first graduates and membership in the North Central Association. With those milestones behind him, Zumberge left Grand Valley in August of 1968 to teach geology at the University of Arizona. He later served as president of Southern Methodist University and the University of Southern California.

Zumberge shows Arnold Ott, Seidman, and George Potter the college's enrollment numbers.

Faculty members Mary Seeger and Wilhelm (Bill) Seeger came to Allendale in 1962 to teach German. They retired from the university in 2005.

The bulk of Grand Valley's history is firmly planted under the leader for the next 32 years – Arend D. (Don) Lubbers. Lubbers was the president of Central College in Pella, Iowa, when Seidman tapped him to be the second president of Grand Valley.

"I've worked hard for Grand Valley," Seidman said. "But the best thing I ever did was recruit Don Lubbers to be the president."

Lubbers took Grand Valley through the Vietnam War protests, financial chaos, and academic restructuring of the early cluster colleges.

"People ask me since I retired in 2001, 'What is your greatest accomplishment?' And I tell them, 'Survival,'" Lubbers said.

Lubbers served as president of Grand Valley from 1969-2001.

Arend D. Lubbers and his wife, Nancy, are pictured with (left to right) John, Mary and Don Jr., on the Allendale Campus.

The volatile 1960s brought protests to Grand Valley although the campus itself offered calmer debate.

Former U.S. President Gerald R. Ford visits with Lubbers, 1977. Ford was a strong supporter of Grand Valley.

While surviving as president in an academic environment for 32 years is a feat unto itself, Lubbers did so much more and, consequently, so did Grand Valley, and so did the region.

He clung to the liberal arts core while recognizing that Grand Valley's cluster colleges were not attracting enough students to ensure long-term survival in a financially competitive environment. The idea was to have about 1,500 students in each of the colleges. The cluster colleges were five individual schools, each with its own identity and educational philosophy. (For more on the cluster colleges, see Academic Milestones, Chapter 3.)

At Lubbers' side for the academic challenges was Glenn A. Niemeyer, who started at Grand Valley in 1963 as a faculty member in history and became provost under Lubbers in 1980. Niemeyer served with him until both retired in 2001.

Glenn A. Niemeyer started at Grand Valley as a history professor in 1963; he later became provost and vice president of Academic Affairs. He retired in 2001.

Lubbers and Niemeyer are pictured with Matt McLogan, vice president for University Relations. McLogan joined the university in 1987.

Richard Morton of the *Grand Rapids Press*, left, stands with Ronald F. VanSteeland.

Jean Enright joined Grand Valley in 1987 as executive assistant to the president and secretary to the Board of Trustees. She served in that capacity until retiring in 2004.

Joyce Hecht, longtime development director, addresses the audience at the 2006 Enrichment Dinner, where she received the Arend D. Lubbers Award. Hecht was recruited by Seidman to lead Grand Valley's development office; she served as director for 25 years.

Following retirement, Lubbers, Niemeyer and VanSteeland (left to right) remain connected to the university.

Overseeing the financial life of Grand Valley was Ronald F. VanSteeland, who came to Grand Valley in 1965 for a job in Human Resources. He spent 35 years at Grand Valley, retiring as vice president for Finance and Administration in 2001.

"The three of us looked each other in the eye every day for almost 30 years," said VanSteeland. "Wonderful people joined us along the way – Matt McLogan, Jean Enright, Maribeth Wardrop, Art Hills and others." Wardrop became Grand Valley's first woman vice president when she joined the university in 2000. She succeeded Joyce Hecht as Grand Valley's chief development officer.

Niemeyer credits two factors for the trio's longevity and success. "One was that we had great respect for one another. We enjoyed working with each other; we respected what the other was doing; we had confidence in each other; we knew each other that well. The second factor, I think, was that we had so much invested in this university," he said.

In the 1970s and '80s, Lubbers, Niemeyer and VanSteeland closed the cluster colleges and stabilized the budget to handle the ever-changing state revenues and subsequent appropriations.

"We always resisted the temptation to spend all the resources that were available," VanSteeland said. Many people came to Grand Valley, "because they liked the idea of having to think smart about how operations are managed, being very cautious about adding resources, and wearing many hats."

State and community leaders, including Governor James Blanchard and Grand Rapids Mayor Gerald Helmholdt, join Lubbers for the groundbreaking for the Grand Rapids Campus in 1986.

Grand Valley's efforts to expand into Grand Rapids in the mid-'80s provided tremendous opportunity for financial partnerships for the revitalization of the city.

Amway co-founder and philanthropist Rich DeVos addresses the crowd gathered for the opening of the Richard M. DeVos Center on the Robert C. Pew Grand Rapids Campus, 2000.

These three leaders had a keen sense for where to put the resources they did have, and in the 1980s, they spearheaded a major move for the university – Grand Valley in downtown Grand Rapids.

The market for classes and programs in Grand Rapids was strong in the mid-'80s, and Grand Valley at that time was renting space there for evening classes. The downtown area needed rejuvenating, and Grand Valley needed to be a factor in the state's second largest city.

In 1986 the state approved Grand Valley's downtown Grand Rapids Campus. The groundbreaking for the L.V. Eberhard Center was held in May of that year. The following year the state Legislature approved the change from Grand Valley State College to Grand Valley State University. Those years brought more than new buildings and a new name; they ushered in tremendous growth and visibility in a reviving city center.

"Allendale is 12 miles west of downtown Grand Rapids and not seen by a lot of people," reasoned Lubbers. "If you build downtown on the Grand River, you are, in a sense, building a presence. When the Eberhard Center was built, thousands and thousands of people saw Grand Valley. You talk about subliminal advertising."

The university was in a tremendous time of growth. In 1983 Grand Valley began a steady, annual rise in enrollment, resulting in it being the fastest growing university in the state. From 1983 to 2001, enrollment went from 6,710 to 19,762.

This aerial photo of downtown Grand Rapids shows the Beckering Family Carillon Tower, Richard M. DeVos Center and the Peter F. Secchia Hall just west of U.S.-131 and the L.V. Eberhard Center just to the east, 2002.

From left, Mark A. Murray, Interim Provost John Gracki, and Assistant Vice President for Human Resources Scott Richardson walk on the Little Mac Bridge, 2001.

The Robert C. Pew Grand Rapids Campus has continued to expand in size and opportunities. It has given Grand Valley a strong, urban campus that is close to internships at businesses, agencies, hospitals and research centers.

When Lubbers, Niemeyer, and VanSteeland retired in 2001, it created an opportunity for Mark A. Murray to become Grand Valley's third president and usher in a new era for the university. Murray was treasurer for the State of Michigan when he was selected by Grand Valley's Board of Trustees following a nationwide search.

"He has managerial skills with very complex organizations, combined with a passion for leadership, knowledge of the area and of the university," Board Chair Donna Brooks said at the time of Murray's appointment.

Faculty members Jean Nagelkerk and Patrick Thorpe lead a procession across campus to the Fieldhouse for Convocation, 2004.

When he took over the presidency of Grand Valley, Murray was 46 years old and had spent more than 20 years in various state government leadership positions. In addition to state treasurer, he was the education policy advisor to Governor John Engler and had served as state budget director.

"I came in from government, most recently coming from a more conservative administration into a higher education institution," Murray said. "I knew my first job was to sit and visit with the faculty in small groups, and ultimately in larger groups, and get to know them and share what was on my mind as well as my esteem for Grand Valley."

Murray said his initial meetings were going quite well when the unthinkable happened – terrorists attacked the United States. Murray recognized that this was a critical moment of leadership for him. He was thrust into helping the community through the shock and devastation of 9/11. He said he first thought about the students, and that focus carried him through those difficult moments.

"My first thoughts went to the fact that we have literally thousands of young people who have just moved away from home," Murray said. He quickly worked with people on campus to organize a gathering at the Cook Carillon Tower.

"I know that did great good for the campus," Murray said. "It gave us a place to gather, reflect, pray, simply be with each other and give each other the kind of support that is appropriate in that kind of setting."

Murray and Governor Jennifer Granholm talk about the Cool Cities plan in Loosemore Auditorium, 2004.

Murray addresses students, faculty and staff members shortly after the September 11 terrorist attacks, 2001.

The Lakers won back-to-back national football championships. Murray joins players in the locker room in Alabama in 2003 for the team's second triumph and celebration.

Patricia Oldt, left, is recognized at a Board of Trustees meeting for her years of service as vice president for Planning and Equity, 2007. At right is board chair Lucille Taylor.

Murray said one of his goals was to broaden the university's strong image outside of West Michigan. A large marketing restructuring and campaign took place, and a concentration of efforts focused on the southeast side of Michigan. Enrollment figures reflect the university's successful efforts. In 2001, 53 percent of students came from the tri-counties surrounding Grand Valley (Kent, Ottawa, Muskegon) and 47 percent came from outside of them. In fall 2009 that percentage had shifted to 42 percent from the tri-counties and 58 percent from outside the immediate area.

After Murray's first year, it was time to hire a provost. John Gracki, associate vice provost for Academic Affairs, had been serving as interim provost following Niemeyer's retirement. Murray hired Gayle R. Davis and later said, "Gayle came with that passion for undergraduate education, and came with a real depth of love of the academy."

Davis had served as vice president for Academic Affairs and Research at Wichita State University in Kansas before coming to Grand Valley.

"I knew that I needed a strong provost and someone who would thrive in this wonderful community focused on an undergraduate education," said Murray. "Gayle was a delight to work with. She's done enormous good for the university."

Davis said the Grand Valley opportunity was one she could not resist. "It was a new team in an organization that had stability and a young, vibrant university in a place I love. It had a niche in higher education that was very attractive to me at a personal level," she said.

Early on Davis tackled the restructuring of Grand Valley's different academic divisions and units to align them more closely with those of comparable universities. (See Academic Milestones, Chapter 3.)

Grand Valley was certainly changing in size and structure, but what did not change was strategic vision. Murray oversaw the completion and opening of the Cook-DeVos Center for Health Sciences in fall 2003.

The decision to place CHS in the center of what would come to be known as Grand Rapids' "Medical Mile" was genius. Following that decision Murray and the leadership team made sure the university's programs capitalized on the building's location near hospitals and research centers, which would offer internships for students and opportunities for community outreach and partnerships.

Murray marks the opening of the Cook-DeVos Center for Health Sciences by placing a time capsule within the building. Lawmakers and supporters gathered for the celebration of Grand Valley on the 'Medical Mile,' 2003.

Expansion of area medical and research facilities brought construction cranes and activities that continued for years on the 'Medical Mile,' 2009.

Elizabeth Murray and Mark Murray are pictured, 2006.

Murray signs an agreement with the University of Michigan to create a dual bachelor of science/doctor of pharmacy degree program. He is joined by Dean Doug Kindschi (left) and the University of Michigan's College of Pharmacy Dean George Kenyon, 2002.

Murray understood how essential a vibrant community is to attracting the best and the brightest; he also understood Lansing. His knowledge of the state budget was a key reason the board hired him to lead Grand Valley. The university consistently was not, and still is not, funded at the floor level that the Legislature itself said public universities should be. Murray's credibility as the former state treasurer made him a force in Lansing — a force that succinctly outlined the need for change, but a force that was constrained by Michigan's economy.

"One of the things I had the privilege of doing was testifying in front of the state Legislature," Murray said. "I never had to advocate for a particular funding formula. I always said, you pick any public policy that you believe is warranted — undergraduate success, graduation rates, job placement rates — whatever you want to focus on, funding for Grand Valley will improve. The status quo was so unfair. We did make some progress, but unfortunately not enough to get real equity."

In looking back at his time on campus, Murray said he is particularly proud of the growth of the quality and reputation of Grand Valley under his watch. "I really think we had a great team, and I was able to continue to help make this a better institution," recalled Murray. "I think this is an institution where the flywheel was moving very, very fast when I got here, and I was able to keep that flywheel spinning."

Murray's success was duly noted by Meijer Inc., a West Michigan family-owned, superstore chain. In addition to his presidential duties, Murray served on Meijer's Board of Directors, and leaders there recognized his talents. Murray, who said he thrives on challenges, resigned as president of Grand Valley in 2006 to become president of Meijer. So, five years after replacing a president who had been at Grand Valley for 32 years, the Board of Trustees had to do another presidential search. They went back to the academy for their choice.

In July 2006 the Board of Trustees appointed Thomas J. Haas as the university's fourth president. Haas had been president of the State University of New York, Cobleskill. He was a 1973 honors graduate of the U.S. Coast Guard Academy and served two years on the U.S. Coast Guard cutter *Acacia* in Port Huron. He has two master's degrees from the University of Michigan and a doctorate in chemistry from the University of Connecticut.

Haas was steeped in academia, having served as a tenured faculty member, department chair, dean, vice president and president. "His qualities meet the highest standards and leadership criteria set forth by the board," said Donna Brooks, chair of the Presidential Search Advisory Committee and the Board of Trustees, at the time.

Haas is an internationally recognized expert in hazardous material transportation, and in addition to his appointment as president of Grand Valley, he was appointed professor of chemistry. He liked what he found at Grand Valley.

The Board of Trustees introduces Thomas J. Haas and his wife Marcia to the community in 2006 when his appointment as president was announced. Seated are board chair Donna Brooks and board member Jessie Dalman, left.

During Haas' first tour of campus as the newly announced president, a student shouted out the nickname 'T-Haas,' and it became a campus favorite, 2006.

"It was a campus that had a developing reputation for producing quality graduates who were ready for the workforce here in Michigan," Haas said. "The students were ready to assume their responsibilities in leadership, and I think Grand Valley was very appealing because it had dramatically focused on offering programs that are relevant."

Haas said he was attracted to the university's mission statement that includes educating students to shape their lives, their professions, and their societies, and he wanted to be relevant to them. Upon arriving on campus, he made it known he would be looking for pick-up basketball with students in the Fieldhouse and hosting pancake breakfasts for members of Student Senate. On one of his first walks around campus, a large group of students gathered. They began chatting with their new president and asking questions, including, "What should we call you?" One yelled out, "Hey, T-Haas," and the nickname stuck.

Murray hands off the baton and the leadership of Grand Valley to Haas during Haas' Investiture, 2006.

Haas was also stuck with Michigan's poor financial condition, and the situation with state funding would only worsen. Grand Valley was already at the bottom when it came to state appropriations per student. Nonetheless, as a public university, Grand Valley had to meet the financial challenges. With every entity and institution in Michigan scrapping for dollars, Haas commissioned the university's first Accountability Report in 2007.

The annual report is issued to show state legislators, taxpayers, students and parents that Grand Valley is a responsible steward of its resources and shows a great return on investment. The simple but instructive report garnered national attention for its transparency and value and was featured in the Council for Advancement and Support of Education's magazine as a model for other institutions to follow.

Haas said three themes guide him: relevance, stewardship and service, and collectively they lead to academic and building initiatives. "We really attend to the whole nature of the curriculum and the quality of professors that are going to support that curriculum and attract students," said Haas. "Then we have to retain them with quality services. Part of that is in terms of activities, but it's also in terms of the bricks and sticks that support the learning environment."

Under Haas' leadership, Grand Valley began its first doctoral programs, both in the area of health care: Doctor of Nursing Practice and Doctorate of Physical Therapy. Grand Valley dedicated the new Niemeyer Learning and Living Center for the Honors College and named the academic programming after Frederik Meijer.

Haas carries boxes for a student during fall move-in, 2008. Families are met with many 'Helping Hands' and shouldn't be shocked that Grand Valley's current president is among faculty and staff members who report for duty.

A Doctorate of Physical Therapy began under Haas' tenure. Pictured is a physical therapy lab, 2006.

Students gather in Richard M. DeVos Center, 2007.

Frederik Meijer is pleased to endow Grand Valley's Honor's College and its programs during a ceremony marking the naming of the college for him, 2008.

Students in the Kirkhof College of Nursing's first doctoral class stand with faculty members in the Cook-DeVos Center for Health Sciences.

Students celebrate the opening of the new Niemeyer Learning and Living Center, 2008.

Haas created the Inclusion and Equity Division and appointed Jeanne Arnold, left, as its first vice president. Maribeth Wardrop, vice president for Development, is at right.

Haas created an Inclusion and Equity Division with leadership at the vice presidential level, giving Grand Valley a distinction as one of the first universities of its type in the country to do so.

Under Haas the university undertook its first comprehensive campaign. "Shaping Our Future" was announced in June 2008 with a goal of raising $50 million. Co-chairs for the largest initiative in Grand Valley's history were Jim and Donna Brooks and Dan and Pamella DeVos. The top priority remained a new library.

In 2008 it was announced that the university's proposed Learning and Information Commons would be named in memory of Mary Idema Pew. Pew is the late wife of Robert C. Pew II, chairman emeritus of Steelcase Inc., and the daughter of Walter and Mary Idema, also regarded as one of the founding families of Steelcase Inc. Her daughter, Kate Pew Wolters, was president of the board at Grand Valley as the university marked its 50th anniversary.

Pictured is a rendering of the proposed Mary Idema Pew Library Learning and Information Commons.

From left are Jim and Donna Brooks and Pamella and Dan DeVos, chairs of the Shaping Our Future Campaign.

Students walk through the Great Lakes Plaza, which is in the center of the Great Lakes buildings and Zumberge Library, 2007.

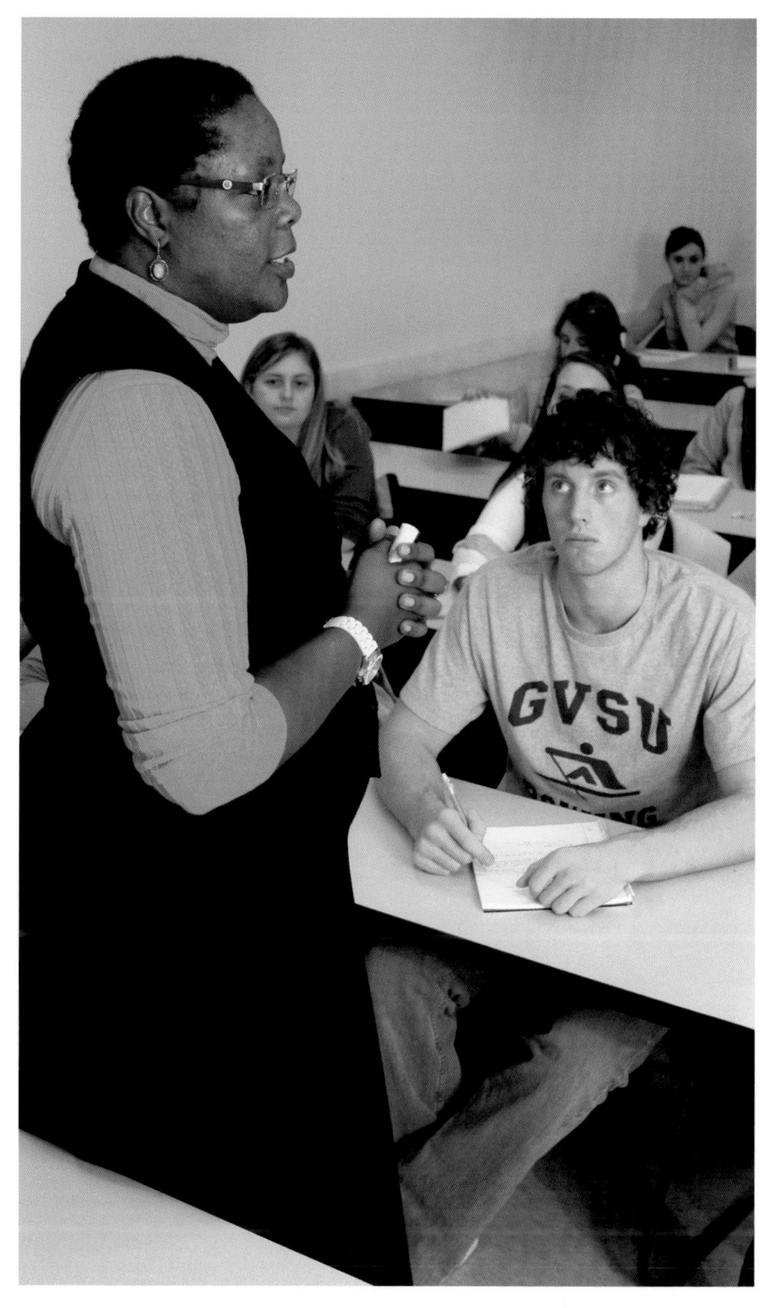

Cheryl Boudreaux, assistant professor of sociology, leads a class, 2008.

Haas took leadership roles outside of the university, working with the North Central Association Higher Learning Commission and the American Council of Education Commission on Effective Leadership, in addition to serving on local boards and chairing the Michigan Public Universities Presidents Council.

His main focus remained Grand Valley and its students, a focus he shared with the campus community. "The faculty and staff here have embraced the mission, embraced our students and understand their role and responsibility in delivering services to students," Haas said. "Those services will give them opportunities to succeed so they can take leadership roles in their communities."

Educating students to shape their lives, their professions, and their societies – Grand Valley's promise continues.

– BY MARY EILLEEN LYON

Haas testifies before the state House Appropriations Subcommittee on Higher Education, saying higher education is a public good and deserving of investment, 2009.

D.J. ANGUS
ALLENDALE
Thank you for
Showing me
the WORLD
LAKE MICHIGAN HALL
COLLEGE
IV
COLLEGE
IV
GRAND VALLEY STATE COLLEGES
GRAND VALLEY
STATE COLLEGES

ACADEMIC MILESTONES

3

WHEN THE MICHIGAN LEGISLATURE approved the establishment of Grand Valley State College in August of 1960, the founders had a vision for a new kind of institution. This new venture would eventually bring about alternative ideas for learning, but one philosophical approach would hold true – liberal education. Throughout Grand Valley's first 50 years, a commitment to offering a liberal education has served as the foundation for all of its academic programs in order to foster critical thinking, creative problem solving and cultural understanding.

Early academic plans called for a college of literature, science and the arts, and a teacher certification curriculum. Members of the pioneer class were required to complete a nine-course foundation program during their freshman year. Additional courses were offered during the following three years so that by the fall of 1966, a complete four-year program was in operation.

Groundbreaking for construction of Grand Valley's first academic building was held in August 1962. Also that year, the first library was set up in the Pink House, a small private house with a two-car garage. The new library was moved to Lake Michigan Hall in 1963. Two learning centers were built for the pioneer class entering in 1963: one contained lecture rooms and faculty offices, while the other made room for science labs, administrative offices and food service.

Students and faculty attend the first convocation in Lake Michigan Hall, 1963.

The Pink House was the first location of Grand Valley's administration offices and library.

The library moved from the Pink House to Lake Michigan Hall in 1963.

A student uses the audio-visual services in a study carrel, equipped with headphones, microphone, video screen and typewriter.

Students shared "study carrels," a storage cabinet for books and supplies and an adjoining clothes locker. The sound-protected carrels were equipped with audio and visual aids to help students perfect language skills and supplement studies in all subjects. The academic year was set up in quarters in which students took three, five-credit classes. Students could choose from several areas of study, including economics, mathematics, chemistry, the sciences, sociology, political science, history, psychology and English literature.

The name College of Arts and Sciences was given to the main unit of studies, and the interdisciplinary School of General Studies was scheduled to open in the fall 1968. On June 18, 1967, the first graduation was held in a tent on the Allendale Campus. The graduating class of 138 included 86 members of the pioneer class.

President James H. Zumberge presents a diploma during the first commencement held in a tent on the Allendale Campus, 1967.

Grand Valley State College was accredited by North Central Association in March 1968, and, soon after, cluster colleges were formed. Part of the original vision, the cluster colleges were five individual schools, each with its own identity and educational philosophy. "The plan was to organize the college around kind of a European cluster college society with 1,500 students in each of the colleges," said Ron VanSteeland, retired vice president for Finance and Administration. The idea would become known as "the great experiment."

The five cluster colleges were as follows:

- College of Arts and Sciences was a traditional liberal arts college;
- Thomas Jefferson College offered a curriculum that encouraged individual study and interdisciplinary learning;
- College III, renamed William James College, offered individualized academic programs with theoretical and practical emphases;
- College IV, later named Kirkhof College, began with a self-paced learning module and evolved into a college of liberal and professional studies;
- F.E. Seidman College of Business, named for Frank Seidman (father of Grand Valley founder L. William Seidman), offered upper-division and graduate business courses.

In 1972 Grand Valley changed its name to Grand Valley State Colleges in recognition of the separate colleges.

Faculty members of College IV gather on the balcony of Lake Superior Hall.

President Arend D. Lubbers looks at a display created by William James College students.

Logos from four of the cluster colleges are pictured.

President Arend D. Lubbers helped establish the colleges. "There was considerable success with these colleges because there were many students who wanted alternative education," said Lubbers. "They attracted excellent students who wanted something different."

William James College was founded on a vocational model, and the curriculum was designed to lead students into the workforce. It evolved into a place where older adults could get their degrees in a vocational setting. Kirkhof College, named for Ottawa County businessman and entrepreneur Russel Kirkhof, was designed for more independent study. Kirkhof gave the first $1 million donation to Grand Valley in 1978.

Grand Valley receives accreditation from the North Central Association, 1968.

Students engage in discussion during class in Lake Huron Hall.

In 1973, the Seidman College of Business offered the first graduate program – the Master of Business Administration – in response to the region's business and industry need for advanced employee development.

Thomas Jefferson College attracted students who wanted something different, more independent study. Its curriculum proved to be too far from the mainstream. Thomas Jefferson College closed in 1978. "Many thought we closed it for financial reasons," said Glenn A. Niemeyer, former provost, "but it was because the academic climate across the country had changed. Things were moving much more in the direction of what was traditional."

After serving 24 years at the Doehler-Jarvis Division of the National Lead Company, Professor Emeritus Earl Harper came to Grand Valley in 1971. He served as assistant dean in the College of Arts and Sciences from 1971-1976 and had two stints as chair of the Management Department from 1979-1986 and 1989-1992.

The economic crisis of the late 1970s made it financially difficult to sustain the remaining colleges. With a change in social attitudes and a decline in enrollment and state appropriations, "the great experiment" was coming to an end. In 1982, the cluster colleges were dissolved for a more traditional organizational structure and were consolidated back under the name Grand Valley State College. "We wanted to protect the liberal arts core and at the same time add professional programs that the region in West Michigan needed," Lubbers said. "Most faculty fit into the new departmental scheme and into a larger College of Arts and Sciences."

As part of the reorganization in 1982, Lubbers began pushing for more graduate programs, like the Master of Education, believing this would be vital to the college's success. Graduate programs were offered in communications, computer science, engineering and public administration. Several professional schools had already formed or were being formed, including the School of Education, School of Social Work, School of Nursing and School of Criminal Justice.

"The image of the university and reputation of the institution had turned around and it was an exciting place to work," said Ronald F. Van Steeland, retired vice president for Finance and Administration. "Admissions had a lot of applicants, an athletic program was initiated and the arts were being supported. We were not only popular to students from West Michigan, but we were beginning to be noticed on the southeastern side of the state."

The Cook-DeVos Center for Health Sciences, which houses Grand Valley's nursing and health professions programs, opened in 2003. It is located on 'Medical Mile' in downtown Grand Rapids.

Pictured is the Frey Foundation Learning Center in the Cook-DeVos Center for Health Sciences. The artwork, 'In Reverence of Remedies' by alumna Julie Upmeyer, is among the top 50 favorite pieces of art from the university's collections.

Discussions began as early as the late '70s and early '80s to create a campus in downtown Grand Rapids. Grand Valley was adding professional programs at a rapid rate, and the market for students was there. "We began to concentrate on building a university that contributed to the welfare of the people of the region and state," Lubbers said. A growth in enrollment, academic programs, facilities and student life led lawmakers to grant university status to Grand Valley in 1987. By then, Grand Valley had become what the Carnegie Foundation would call a "comprehensive university," offering undergraduate as well as professional and select graduate programs.

As part of its mission, Grand Valley actively seeks ways to positively impact public K-12 education. One of those ways is through the authorization of charter schools. In 1995 Grand Valley chartered its first three schools, serving a total of 350 students. By 2010 the university chartered 28 schools and three urban high school academies, serving more than 17,800 students.

Also in 1995 Grand Valley began classes in two regional centers: the Muskegon Regional Center at the Stevenson Center for Higher Education at Muskegon Community College, and the Traverse City Regional Center at the Northwestern Michigan College University Center.

In 2003 under President Mark A. Murray, Grand Valley opened the Cook-DeVos Center for Health Sciences on "Medical Mile" in downtown Grand Rapids. This allowed for the university's health professions programs to be offered in one strategically chosen location.

Noah Creamer, a liberal studies major, celebrates his graduation at commencement in Traverse City with his daughter, Sierra, and one of his instructors, Susan Odgers.

Grand Valley began offering courses and degree programs at the Traverse City Regional Center in 1995. The commencement ceremony focuses on the graduates and their families, as many graduates are non-traditional students.

Student Adam Falk plays catch with a child in Ghana during a study abroad trip in 2008. Falk attended classes at the University of Cape Coast, one of Grand Valley's partner institutions.

Grand Valley's first foreign university partnership was established in Krakow, Poland, in 1977. Today, the university's Barbara H. Padnos International Center offers more than 4,000 study abroad programs. Grand Valley is consistently ranked within the top 10 schools in the country for student participation with more than 600 students who study abroad annually.

Gayle R. Davis, provost and vice president for Academic Affairs, receives the Distinguished Woman in Higher Education Leadership Award from the Michigan American Council on Education Network, 2009.

LearnLab classrooms in the Frederik Meijer Honors College include projection screens to make learning interactive. Students access notes through their laptops, and professors use a copycam to send information to students.

The university continued to set enrollment records and increase its areas of study. Upon completion of the 2003 Strategic Plan during Murray's early years, another major reorganization was necessary. When Gayle R. Davis came to Grand Valley in 2002 as provost and vice president of Academic Affairs, she undertook a complete reorganization of the university's academic units. Davis said the new plan, implemented in the fall of 2004, would enable the university to advance its mission with an organizational structure that would facilitate achievement of its goals.

Enrollment numbers reached nearly 7,000 by 1980, 11,000 by 1990 and 20,000 in 2002. Grand Valley's academic reputation grew, and the number of freshman applications continued to increase. Davis said the reorganization reaffirmed the university's commitment to liberal education as the foundation for all liberal arts and sciences disciplines as well as interdisciplinary studies and professional studies at the undergraduate and graduate levels.

"Grand Valley is known for its wide array of strong programs, small class sizes and its student-centered, academically rigorous environment, facts that attract the very best students," said Davis. For the past several years, including 2010, Grand Valley has been named a "Best in the Midwest" college by the Princeton Review Company, selected on the basis of its excellent academic programs and student comments about the university. Every year from 1996-2010, Grand Valley has been named one of "America's 100 Best College Buys" by Institutional Research and Evaluation Inc.

One of the major changes brought on by the reorganization was, for the second time in Grand Valley's history, the establishment of a College of Liberal Arts and Sciences, which combined the traditional departments in the former divisions of Arts and Humanities, Science and Mathematics and Social Sciences.

The major professional programs moved out of their divisions and gained needed autonomy for their various missions. In all, seven other colleges were named: Seidman College of Business, College of Community and Public Service, College of Education, Padnos College of Engineering and Computing, College of Health Professions, Kirkhof College of Nursing and the College of Interdisciplinary Studies. A reminder of Grand Valley's innovative spirit, the College of Interdisciplinary Studies serves as a place for collaborative work that spans more than one college of the university.

The Grand Valley Board of Trustees continued to plan for the future by approving a refreshed version of the University Strategic Plan in July 2007 under the direction of President Thomas J. Haas. "The plan provides direction and offers a road map for the institution to follow. It is designed for improving every aspect of Grand Valley's performance as we continue to mature as an institution," said Haas.

Members of the Strategic Positioning Committee updated the plan for 2010-2015 to support Grand Valley's vision to become recognized as one of the nation's premiere Carnegie classification "Master's Large" institutions of higher education grounded in the tradition of liberal education.

– BY DOTTIE BARNES

In 2009 Grand Valley marked its 25th year as host to the Region 12 Michigan Science Olympiad. Grand Valley was chosen to host the national tournament in 1998.

William F. Pickard, chairman and CEO of VITEC in Detroit, addresses a class on entrepreneurship, 2009. Pickard was a member of Grand Valley's Board of Control from 1977-1988. A living center is named for him on the Allendale Campus.

CENTERS OF EXCELLENCE

ANNIS WATER RESOURCES INSTITUTE

The Robert B. Annis Water Resources Institute is a multidisciplinary research organization committed to the study of freshwater resources. The institute, established in 1986, occupies the Lake Michigan Center on Muskegon Lake in Muskegon and includes classrooms, conference areas, analytical labs and research labs. AWRI operates its own research vessels, the *D.J. Angus* and the *W.G. Jackson*, and offers the Water Resources Outreach Education Program for K-12 schools and community groups. The institute receives millions of dollars in state and federal grant awards for the study of Michigan lakes and rivers. Ronald Ward was the institute's first director; he retired in 2001 and was replaced by Alan D. Steinman.

DOROTHY A. JOHNSON CENTER FOR PHILANTHROPY

The Center for Philanthropy began in 1992 as a multidisciplinary, university-wide center, developed with the support of the W.K. Kellogg Foundation. In 1999 it was renamed to honor Dorothy A. Johnson (shown below) and her distinguished career.

The Johnson Center serves the needs of the nonprofit and philanthropic sectors with initiatives like the Community Research Institute, The Grantmaking School and *The Foundation Review*. The center's first director was Thom Jeavons, followed by Dorothy Freeman and Donna VanIwaarden. Kathy A. Agard was named executive director in 2006.

VAN ANDEL GLOBAL TRADE CENTER

Founded in 1999, the Van Andel Global Trade Center was established in response to needs identified by the business, academic and economic development communities. Named for Jay Van Andel, co-founder of Amway, the center was established as a core facility dedicated to advancing global trade and supporting West Michigan businesses as they prepare to enter and prosper in the era of international business.

Since its inception, the center has provided international training to more than 14,000 individuals and assisted 870 companies with international consulting projects through its community outreach.

The center named Jeffrey Meyer executive director in 1999; Sonja Johnson was named executive director in 2008 after serving as interim director for two years.

HAUENSTEIN CENTER FOR PRESIDENTIAL STUDIES

The Hauenstein Center for Presidential Studies, inspired by Ralph W. Hauenstein's (above left) life of leadership and service, has become one of the leading presidential studies centers in the nation. Established in 2001, the center has hosted more than 275 programs: four were broadcast by C-SPAN and three others were Webcast to an international audience. Richard Norton Smith was named part-time director in 2001. Patricia Oldt, vice president for Planning and Equity, served as interim director from 2001 until Gleaves Whitney was named the center's first full-time director in 2003.

The center's Peter C. Cook Leadership Academy is dedicated to inspiring, informing and connecting high-potential leaders at Grand Valley who are committed to serving their community, state and nation. Cook is pictured above, right.

THE MICHIGAN ALTERNATIVE AND RENEWABLE ENERGY CENTER

MAREC was developed in 2003 as a direct response to the growing need for alternative and renewable energy sources. MAREC is becoming an international destination point for researchers and businesses developing alternative energy technologies and applications. The center, located in the Muskegon Lakeshore SmartZone, is also a leading resource for education and instruction on alternative energy.

MAREC is a self-sustaining distributive energy center that features photovoltaic solar roof tiles, a micro turbine and a wind turbine. In addition, the facility offers business incubator space, an energy laboratory, a conference center and classroom facilities. MAREC is one of two SmartZones designated by the state. Inventor Imad Mahawili was named MAREC's first executive director in 2003; he was replaced by T. Arnold (Arn) Boezaart in 2009.

WEST MICHIGAN SCIENCE AND TECHNOLOGY INITIATIVE

A second Grand Valley SmartZone, founded in 2003, is the West Michigan Science and Technology Initiative. It grew from investments by Grand Valley, the Michigan Economic Development Corporation and the Local Development Authority.

Its partners include Grand Valley, Van Andel Research Institute, City of Grand Rapids, Grand Rapids Community College, The Right Place Inc., Spectrum Health, Saint Mary's Health Care, Mary Free Bed Rehabilitation Hospital and Grand Angels.

The initiative has assisted more than 400 clients in commercialization of new products and has helped secure $9 million in federal and state grants.

Matt Dugener served as executive director from 2003-2007. Linda Chamberlain replaced him until 2010 when she was named director of Seidman College of Business' Center for Entrepreneurship and Innovation.

GVSC
1967
STREET ACADEMY
International Club

STUDENT LIFE

4

THE LEARNING THAT TAKES PLACE inside the classroom is a large part of higher education. But at a place like Grand Valley, there is much learning that happens informally – while chatting over coffee, attending a concert, volunteering or simply letting off steam.

Throughout Grand Valley's 50 years, students have found a breathtaking array of ways to spend their time outside the classroom.

Nancee Miller – an early Grand Valley student who would later become Alumni Relations director – spoke of the excitement of blazing a new trail. "There was a sense of adventure," Miller said. "There was an opportunity to establish something, and to be part of something at the beginning, and, quite frankly, that underlying current was part of my undergraduate years. We decided on the colors of the university: blue, black and white. There was a contest to name the athletic mascot, the Laker."

Pioneer student Diane Paton said, in the early days, Grand Valley students were largely responsible for creating their own activities. "In the beginning it was tough. There was not a lot to do," she said, mentioning activities like powder-puff football, ice sculptures and lots of card games.

KEYSTONE

CLUBS ORGANIZED AT GVSC

First Mixer Succeeds

Party Invitation Extended

The Choir Needs You

Need Money Anyone?

KEYSTONE

Jellema To Speak Today

Dance Support Falters

Bookstore To Open In Spring Quarter

Twirp Season Arrives

Carrels Finished!

Progress Reported

Stay Away 'til Opening Day

Dykstras Host Committee

HOOTENANNY RECAPS

The *Keystone* was Grand Valley's first student-run newspaper. Established in 1963, it was succeeded by the *Valley View* from 1966-1968 and then the award-winning *Lanthorn* from 1968 to the present. These early issues of the *Keystone* focused on peculiar features of student culture of the time, including big folk music sing-a-longs called hootenannies.

The first issue of the student newspaper, the *Keystone*, was published November 22, 1963 – the same day President John F. Kennedy was assassinated – and continued through 1966. During that first year, it documented many milestones: building openings, faculty hirings, the first formal dance and arrival of the Beatles in the U.S.

"Grand Valley State College is more than a name, a plan, a dream; it is a reality," wrote Elaine Rosendall in the first issue of the *Keystone*. "Student government has been organized, parties planned, clubs formed, friendships made, impressions built." Among the clubs formed were a gun club, a ski club and Inter-Varsity Christian Fellowship.

The *Keystone* was succeeded by the *Valley View* (1966-1968) and the *Lanthorn* in 1968. That publication gave President Arend D. Lubbers one of his first job-related headaches. Thanks to some rough language, Ottawa County issued an injunction to close the paper, and its editor was charged with distribution of an obscene publication.

"I remember it was such a crisis that the board members invited me to come here and meet with them before I was due to take the job to talk about strategy and how we should handle this crisis, because we were in real trouble with the public of West Michigan, with the four-letter words," Lubbers said. In 1969 the Michigan Attorney General issued an opinion that the county's injunction was in violation of the First Amendment.

In Grand Valley's early days, freshmen wore beanies at the start of the academic year.

Opened in 1973 Kirkhof Center serves as a gathering place for students.

Students admire a winter carnival ice sculpture.

Smoking wasn't always banned in lecture halls.

The first student center on campus was Seidman House; it opened in 1966.

Students demonstrate in favor of continuing a U.S. presence in Vietnam.

Starting in 1966, students frolicked in the cold during the Winter Carnival. Typical activities included ice sculptures, a beard-growing contest, donkey basketball, dog sled races and a talent show. The beauty contest portion of the talent show was discontinued in 1971 because it "aroused much indignation among women's liberation members on campus," according to GVSC *Student Life Magazine*, which published one issue that year.

The students weren't only concerned with having fun, though. Many were concerned about the war in Vietnam. Lubbers said Grand Valley's openness helped the institution avoid some of the strife that occurred at other campuses around the country. "During the greatest time of protest during the Vietnam War, there were some of the student leaders at Thomas Jefferson College who were certainly on the left side of the political spectrum but who did not want Grand Valley to be shut down or to be torn apart by radicals," he said.

Faculty members show their concern during a protest against the war.

Arend D. Lubbers said Grand Valley's openness helped the campus avoid some of the strife that occurred at other colleges during the Vietnam War.

Students walk on campus between their classes in the mid-1970s.

By the early 1970s Grand Valley's unique cluster college system resulted in an environment of originality. "There was an amazing amount of creativity going on," said Mark Schrock, a William James College student and musician who played with the noted Grand Valley-centered bluegrass band Cabbage Crik. "The staff there was so creative and young and vibrant and hip. It was very cool. And I met people who are still among my closest friends – including my wife."

Serving as the nerve center for student activities, the Campus Center opened in 1973 and was later renamed Russel H. Kirkhof Center. Some features of Kirkhof have remained, including the bookstore and lower-level dining area. But some things changed; for instance, the introduction of the Walkman in the early '80s made the cassette listening lounge obsolete.

Cabbage Crik opens for a little-known Jimmy Buffett in the Campus Center, 1974.

Students taking a break, circa 1970.

Kirkhof Center has undergone three expansions since it was first constructed in 1973.

Freddie Hubbard

Music played a large role in the student life of the 1970s, thanks to an impressive array of national acts who played in the original Fieldhouse, commonly known as the Dome. A short list of artists who passed through Allendale in the '70s includes Aerosmith, Ted Nugent, Bob Seger, Lou Reed, Dr. John, Sly and the Family Stone, Genesis, Curtis Mayfield, the Eagles, Santana, REO Speedwagon and Frank Zappa.

Ted Nugent

Bob Seger (left) and Alto Reed

Dennis DeYoung of Styx

Steve Miller

Throughout the 1970s Grand Valley hosted an annual Blues and Jazz Festival. The festival attracted top national acts.

Jeff Brown, a Grand Valley alumnus who became a staff member, was in charge of bringing music to campus. "I looked at the whole process as a learning lab for students," he said. "It was my job to bring in these acts, but it was the student volunteers who made it all happen. People on campus were just excited to be involved. They would volunteer to do just about any task if it meant they could be in on music somehow. It didn't hurt that you could get a free ticket and one for a friend if you helped out."

Famous psychedelic poster artist Gary Grimshaw created this poster for Curtis Mayfield's performance.

In 1983 Bob Stoll took a job at Grand Valley as coordinator of student activities. As director of the Student Life Office at Grand Valley's 50th anniversary, Stoll has had a front-row seat for many changes at the university.

"The program had a very small budget. It was just a two-person office. There wasn't near the complexity that there is now," Stoll said of his early days.

At that time Student Senate was comprised of 30 students who handled both programming and student government functions. One of the first things Stoll did was to propose to separate those two tasks so the Student Senate could focus on government tasks. The newly created programming board morphed into what is now known as Spotlight Productions.

Willie Nelson plays a concert in the Fieldhouse, 1982.

Longtime Director of Student Life Bob Stoll started his tenure at Grand Valley in 1983.

Students race canoes on Zumberge Pond during a spring festival, circa 1978.

The Presidents' Ball is a long-standing and popular tradition. It outgrew its former Kirkhof Center home and is held at the DeVos Place Convention Center in Grand Rapids.

One of the first casualties of the separation was the Blues and Jazz Festival, which ended in 1983. "We were spending a third of the Student Life dollars on that one event," Stoll said. "It was a great event, but the resources were needed in other areas."

Stoll said it was important to spread the funding around and build a community rather than focus on periodic large-scale events. "There weren't any real huge traditions," Stoll said. "That was one of the things we lacked as a campus."

One long-standing Grand Valley tradition, the annual formal Presidents' Ball, began in 1986. Hosted each year by Grand Valley's president and the Student Senate president, it provides a chance for students to get all dressed up and dance the night away. It started off in the Kirkhof Center's Grand River Room, eventually taking up all three floors of the building. The event attracted 300 attendees in the first few years.

Over time, the Presidents' Ball moved to Welsh Auditorium, Grand Rapids Public Museum, and then the Eberhard Center. In its current home at the DeVos Place Convention Center, some 500 people attend the dinner and 4,000 people attend the dance.

Each ball has a theme; in recent years, those themes were "A Red Carpet Affair," "A Roman Triumph" and "An Evening of Crystal Elegance." Preceding the dance is an awards ceremony honoring recipients of the Presidential Appreciation Award, Distinguished Individual of the Year Award and the Student Award for Faculty Excellence.

As the university continued to grow, it became apparent that more room was needed for student organizations. Kirkhof Center was the hub, but by the end of the '90s it was overtaxed. In 2002 a renovation and addition to Kirkhof Center were completed. One of the features was a new Student Organization Center, providing office space for registered student groups, which by 2009 numbered nearly 300. A 2008 renovation added space for three student services centers: the Lesbian, Gay, Bisexual and Transgender Resource Center, the Office of Multicultural Affairs and the Women's Center.

The additional space reflected the needs of a student community that had changed dramatically since Grand Valley's inception. Stoll said the goal when he first arrived was simply to try and keep people on campus.

"At first, the challenge was to try and make this a place where people would want to stay, so we worked on establishing services, programs and entertainment. We've accomplished that on many fronts," Stoll said. "I always laugh when people say there's nothing to do. There are so many things going on here."

Student Life has evolved to keep up with student needs. Now, even "down time" is frequently learning time. "The outcomes are much more intentional than they used to be," Stoll said.

Kirkhof Center wasn't the only student-centered facility that received an upgrade over time. People who remember the old-style college dorms may be surprised at the high-quality housing Grand Valley has built in recent years.

"We went from two students to a room with a bathroom down the hall to apartments with a kitchen, bedroom and dishwasher. So we've gone from housing students to creating communities that have all the conveniences of home," said Andy Beachnau, director of Housing, Residence Life and Health Services.

Cassonya Carter-Pugh, center, has led the Voices of GVSU, a gospel choir, since 1987 when she was a student. The active student organization performs year-round at campus and area events.

Family Weekend traditionally falls on a home football weekend.

Students and supporters of the LGBT Resource Center are pictured. Since 2008 the center's permanent location has been Kirkhof Center.

The Intercultural Festival, formerly known as the Ethnic Festival, is a celebration of cultures from around the world.

Students sit beneath 'The Mouse Trap' in Kirkhof Center. The painting by Andy Twietmeyer is one of the top 50 favorite pieces of art from the university's collections.

Student Senate is one avenue for students who want to make a positive impact on campus. "I think Student Senate can affect students in different ways," said two-term Student Senate president Frank Foster in 2008. "We have about 25 university committees – anything from parking to curriculum – that we sit on. So their voice is represented in those meetings by us."

Stoll said in recent years he's seen a rising sense of social consciousness among students. "When students get here, they're much more civically in tune," he said. "There's a sense of being good stewards of the earth. I've seen that shift in our students."

Instead of spending carefree days on sunny beaches, some Grand Valley students choose to spend their time off helping others. In 2008 Grand Valley's Alternative Breaks program was named the best in the country at the national Break Away Conference. The student organization sends hundreds of GVSU students around the country each year to volunteer over weekends, holiday and spring breaks. Participants travel to work on issues such as community health, affordable housing, animal rights, youth, poverty, and to help people with special needs.

One of the student organizers said his experience was life-changing. "I think participating in Alternative Breaks has been the catalyst for great personal growth," said Geoff Hickox, who participated for four years before becoming the coordinator. "Before, I never volunteered at all; I was centered on my own life. This experience opened up my eyes to a lot of social issues I wasn't aware of."

– BY BRIAN J. BOWE

Kleiner Commons is open 24-hours, seven days a week. Housing Director Andy Beachnau said the hours accommodate today's students.

Members of the Student Senate are sworn into office during a meeting in the Kirkhof Center, 2009.

SEPTEMBER 11: MAKING A COMMUNITY

The Grand Valley community came together when terrorists struck the United States on September 11, 2001. The university was just beginning a new academic year under a new president. Mark A. Murray had been on the job for a little more than two months. Out of the tragedy arose a feeling of community, as more than 4,000 people came together around the Cook Carillon tower with less than 90 minutes notice on that day.

"I ask that you commit yourselves to supporting one another," Murray told the crowd. "As we gather here, great acts of courage and compassion are occurring at the sites of these tragedies. So too, we must demonstrate our courage and compassion. Speak with each other. Share your views. Learn from each other. We are a community and must commit ourselves to supporting each other."

The Grand
TV Auction
Mr Steak
KIDS AUCTION
1983

ARTS AND CULTURE

5

WHEN CLASSES BEGAN AT GRAND VALLEY IN 1963, with more than 260 students, Arthur C. Hills was the only fine arts faculty member. Hills, associate professor of music, was charged by President James H. Zumberge with the responsibility of developing a fine arts program. This charge marked the beginning of a long commitment to fine and performing arts at Grand Valley, a tradition that has continued with each successive president to the benefit of the entire West Michigan community.

MUSIC

One of Hills' first tasks was to organize interested members of the pioneer class into a fledging vocal ensemble called the Singers, later renamed the Grand Valley Singers. Soon after Hills organized the first Arts on Campus Weekend, an annual spring series of events designed to showcase Grand Valley's commitment to the arts. Within a year, Hills took on administrative roles at Grand Valley that would accumulate during his 24 years of service. One example of his many lasting contributions is the university's alma mater, "Hail to Thee Grand Valley," written by Hills in the early '60s.

'GRAND VALLEY ALMA MATER'

by Arthur C. Hills

Hail to thee Grand Valley — We're loyal, steadfast, true.

Praise our Alma Mater — We pledge our faith to you.

Keep your banners flying, black and white and blue.

We sing to thee Grand Valley. United we're for you!

Folk singers Caroline and Sandy Paton perform in Seidman House.

Early concerts were often held in Seidman House, with its seating capacity of 100 stretched to the max. In 1966 tiny dramas began to be performed in Lake Huron Hall in an area that often doubled as a classroom. Once Grand Valley established the cluster colleges in 1967, arts and performance groups grew rapidly. By 1968 Grand Valley State College Friends of the Arts was established to organize and sponsor scholarships, exhibits, lectures and art events for the West Michigan community.

When Arend D. Lubbers succeeded Zumberge as president in 1969, he brought a visionary desire for a preeminent program of arts and culture at Grand Valley. In order to house numerous cultural activities, he directed the construction of the Alexander Calder Fine Arts Center (later renamed the Performing Arts Center), which was completed in 1971. It became a hub for campus artistic presentations with the 500-seat Louis Armstrong Theatre, and support areas such as art studios, music rooms, offices, and theater costume, practice and makeup rooms.

Arthur C. Hills, Grand Valley's first fine arts faculty member, conducts the pioneer class Singers.

Wayne Dunlap, music department chair, arrives in 1971 to spearhead a new direction in curriculum and degree offerings. By spring 1978 the department was offering full degree programs.

The Seven Centuries Singers, a madrigal ensemble at Grand Valley, performed a repertoire of chamber music from medieval to contemporary.

Standing on the balcony of their home, William Root and his wife Natalie are treated to a surprise serenade for their 33rd wedding anniversary by 70 members of the Grand Valley Marching Band. Root established the marching band in 1976, and retired at age 60, after 10 years at Grand Valley.

The Cook-DeWitt Center is home to the 32-rank Reuter pipe organ.

The 250-seat Cook-DeWitt Center was dedicated on November 24, 1991. The auditorium was designed with enhanced acoustics, particularly for its custom-made 32-rank Reuter concert pipe organ, donated by Jay and Betty Van Andel. To celebrate the inspiring sounds of the concert organ, an "Inaugural Series" of organ recitals continued through April 1992.

Ellen Pool, recently honored for her 25 years of service to Grand Valley, directs the Arts Chorale, Select Women's Ensemble and the Cantate Chamber Ensemble. The 60-voice Arts Chorale has become a key presence on campus and in the community, including performances with the Grand Rapids Symphony.

The University Arts Chorale, directed by Ellen Pool, has performed by invitation with the Grand Rapids Symphony Orchestra.

Music chair from 1984-1996, Julianne Vanden Wyngaard refined the course and degree offerings and worked to procure accreditation from the National Association of the Schools of Music. Together with Lubbers, she was instrumental in the 1994 installation of the Cook Carillon Tower in Allendale and the Beckering Family Carillon on the Robert C. Pew Grand Rapids Campus in 2000. She was named University Carillonneur in 2008.

In 1997 Sherman Van Solkema was named chair of the music department. He established Grand Valley's dance program and invited Jefferson Baum (whose father William Baum taught political science for 40 years at GVSU) to join the faculty. Since its inception, the program has grown to include three full-time faculty members who oversee a bachelor's degree program in dance. The Baum family's commitment to the arts at Grand Valley was further honored in 1998 when Lubbers authorized an endowed fund for the William Baum Lecture Series, which alternates bi-annual piano performances with political science lectures.

Van Solkema also directed a renovation and expansion of the Calder Arts Center. The 1997 project added 14 more teaching studios, a music technology center and a 100-seat performance hall. Now the Performing Arts Center, this well-known artistic hub was renamed when the Department of Art and Design moved to its current location, taking the Calder Fine Arts Center name. Upon his retirement in 2001, a hall in the Performing Arts Center was named the Sherman Van Solkema Recital Hall.

University Carillonneur Julianne Vanden Wyngaard stands with one of the 48 bells cast for the Beckering Family Carillon, landmark structure of the Robert C. Pew Grand Rapids Campus, dedicated in 2000. The Cook Carillon Tower, on the Allendale Campus, was dedicated on November 15, 1994.

Dance is a popular program in the Department of Music.

Grand Valley Opera Theatre began in 1998 with a production of 'Amahl and the Night Visitors.'

In 1998 a production of "Amahl and the Night Visitors" introduced the campus community to the newly formed Grand Valley Opera Theatre, directed by Dale Schriemer. Laura Gardner Salazar, whose long career at Grand Valley included more than 60 stage productions, was stage director for this production. Each year Opera Theatre alternates productions of opera and musical theater.

In 2006 Danny Phipps was named chair of music and dance. Under his leadership the department has grown to more than 30 full-time faculty members and 300 music majors and minors.

Current degree programs are now fully accredited and include three bachelor's degree programs. Students participate in numerous ensembles, such as the GVSU Symphony Orchestra, Symphonic Wind Ensemble, Early Music Ensemble, University Arts Chorale, Varsity Men's Choir, Dance Ensemble and the award-winning New Music Ensemble.

Sherman Van Solkema

Danny Phipps

Grand Valley's cultural presence in downtown Grand Rapids was established in the 1970s with an experimental theater, Stage 3, once located in a former church.

THEATER

In 1972 an experimental storefront theater, named Stage 3, was established in a former shoe store on Campau Avenue. The location was selected to provide a Grand Valley performing arts presence in downtown Grand Rapids offering contemporary and experimental drama not found elsewhere in the area. The program merged with Grand Valley's Thomas Jefferson College in 1973. In 1976 the successful enterprise, directed by Michael Birtwistle, moved to the former Holy Trinity Greek Orthodox Church and opened with Woody Allen's "Play It Again Sam." When the building was sold, performances were moved to the Louis Armstrong Theatre on the Allendale Campus. In 1982 programs and facilities previously under Thomas Jefferson College and the College of Arts and Sciences were consolidated into the current theatre program in the School of Communications.

Establishing cultural diversity within the season of theater performances became a priority in 1992. Since then one major show each year addresses cultural diversity or some cultural conflict. It also enabled diverse collaborations with other areas on campus, from ethnic studies to regional studies to community outreach, and with guest cultural experts. Playwright Elizabeth Wong was brought from Los Angeles to campus for the 1998 production, "Letters to a Student Revolutionary," about the 1989 Tiananmen Square conflict.

Professor Roger Ellis and Professor Emerita Laura Gardener Salazar started Michigan's oldest and largest Shakespeare Festival at Grand Valley in 1993.

The festival has grown to include a Renaissance Faire, an annual Shakespeare stage production, a national Shakespeare scholar-in-residence, who also provides a public lecture, and educational outreach efforts, including young audiences brought to campus and the Bard to Go program. Founded by Professor Karen Libman and others in 2001, BTG takes a touring production to Michigan middle and high school students who might be unable to attend a full Shakespeare production.

Students Kirsten Ellison and Dustin Mason perform a scene from 'Taming of the Shrew.'

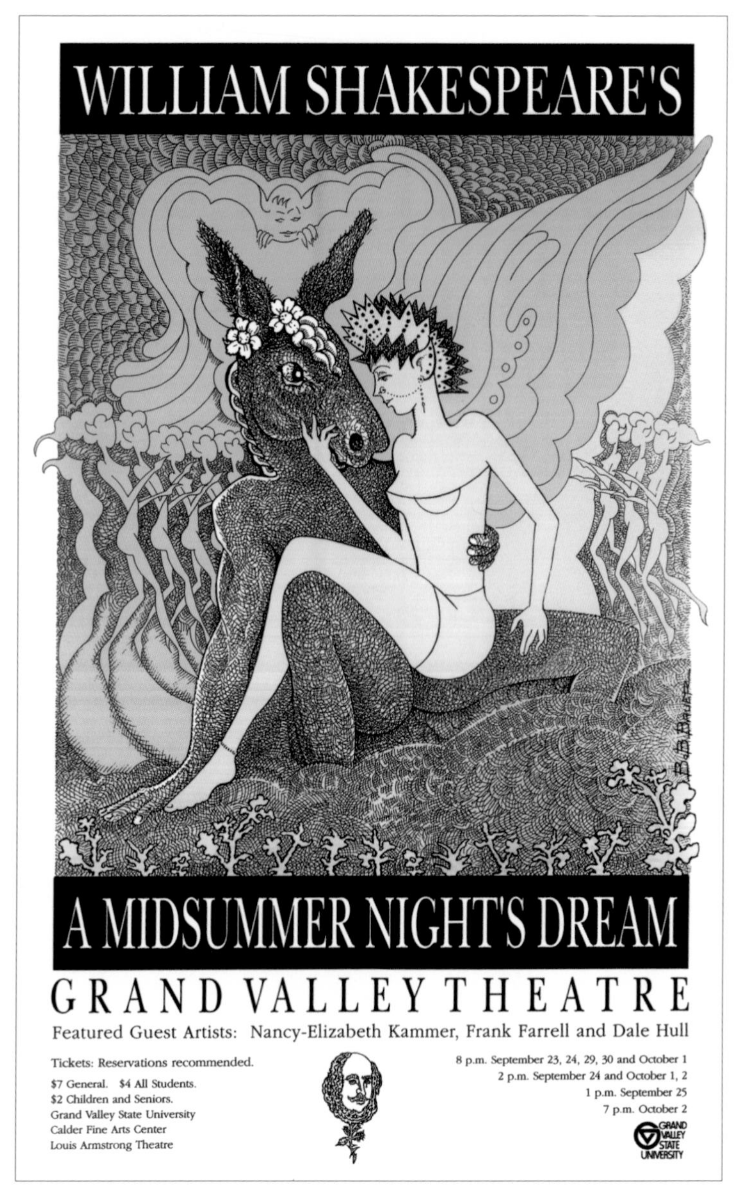

Poster from the 1994 Shakespeare Festival.

A scene from 'Mother Courage and Her Children,' 2002.

Libman has taken BTG students to Jamaica and China, as part of theater's global outreach. The first global venture was in 1998 when Salazar and Ellis took a group of students to Caracas, Venezuela.

Artistic integrity and high quality are paramount in the costume shop. Costume designer Jill Hamilton counts the 2002 production of Bertold Brecht's "Mother Courage and Her Children" among the most challenging, with dozens of uniforms needed for the 100-Year, Revolutionary, Civil and World wars.

'Bard to Go: Kissing and Courting' receives the Best Performance Award at the Sapperlot International Festival of Youth Theatre in Italy, 2009.

In 2009 many former members of the United Stage theater group from Thomas Jefferson College returned for a reunion at the Pew Grand Rapids Campus. Bob Moyer, former Grand Valley instructor, directed a performance of 'United Stage Revisited,' a re-enactment of the story theater the group did decades before, pictured above.

West Michigan's first local production of 'Rent' was held in 2009 on the Allendale Campus. It was a joint venture between Grand Valley and Heritage Theatre Group in Grand Rapids; Manley Pope was guest director.

ART GALLERIES AND COLLECTIONS

Lubbers realized how important the space in which people work and live affects how they do it, and he had an affinity for meaningful architecture well appointed with works of art. Beginning in 1987, he decided to include art in every new building built on Grand Valley's campuses. A series of outdoor sculptures was installed in 1990 throughout the new South Campus Courtyard, located between the Zumberge Library and the expanded Au Sable Hall.

Enlisting the help of Jean Enright, his executive assistant and secretary to the board, Lubbers continued to purchase art created by faculty members and local artists to expand the university's collection. By the time Henry Matthews was hired as director of galleries and collections in 1998, the collection included more than 700 pieces. Matthews brought a systematic and professional approach to growing the collection and refurbished the main art gallery, located in the Performing Arts Center.

He organized and supervised the committees that select art for each new building. The DeVos Center became a highly visible downtown Grand Rapids showcase and was appointed with more than 400 pieces of art throughout its 270,000 square feet. Included was the first donation by George and Barbara Gordon of 36 works by Grand Rapids' own Mathias J. Alten. That collection, housed in a gallery that bears their names, grew to more than 60 Alten works by 2008.

'Transformational Link,' designed by Detroit artist Gary Kulak, a 45-foot-tall sculpture, stands at the end of the courtyard leading to the bridge over the ravine that cuts the campus into north and south portions.

'Heaven and Earth' by former faculty member James Clover, a 40-foot sculpture weighing 15,000 pounds and crafted over an eight-month period, sits outside Zumberge Library.

Anita Gileo and George Gordon examine the final self-portrait by West Michigan painter Mathias J. Alten in the expanded George and Barbara Gordon Gallery in the DeVos Center.

The Gordon Gallery doubled in size in 2008 to feature more works by Alten.

Additional galleries were established to exhibit the university's growing collections: Red Wall Gallery in Lake Ontario Hall, Faculty/Staff Dining Room Gallery in Kirkhof Center, Eberhard Center Gallery, and exhibit space on the Holland Campus. In addition, the Padnos Student Art and Design Gallery, in Calder Art Center, is devoted exclusively to student work and provides opportunities for students to learn gallery operations.

Major gifts to the university expanded the collection to more than 9,000 pieces of art by 2009. Also that year the entire collection was digitized; it is available online for academic studies and viewing from anywhere in the world.

The annual DeVos Art Lecture began when Loosemore Auditorium was completed on the Pew Grand Rapids Campus. It began by focusing on one of Grand Valley's own artists or collections and has expanded to bring in cultural icons from across the country. John Berry, a Michigan designer long associated with Herman Miller, presented the 2009 lecture. Two of Grand Valley's first ladies, Elizabeth Murray and Marcia Haas, have served as the honorary chair of the lecture series.

50 FAVORITE PIECES OF ART

In honor of Grand Valley's 50th anniversary, 50 favorite pieces of art from the university's galleries and collections were selected by public opinion. They represent the wide range of artists, media and subjects found in the university's collections, which number more than 9,000 works.

They also reflect the talents of faculty members, students and alumni as well as the generosity of hundreds of art donors and arts communities internationally. Art is located throughout all of Grand Valley's campuses and every building, including in classrooms.

2 Place Lamartine
Terence La Noue, American

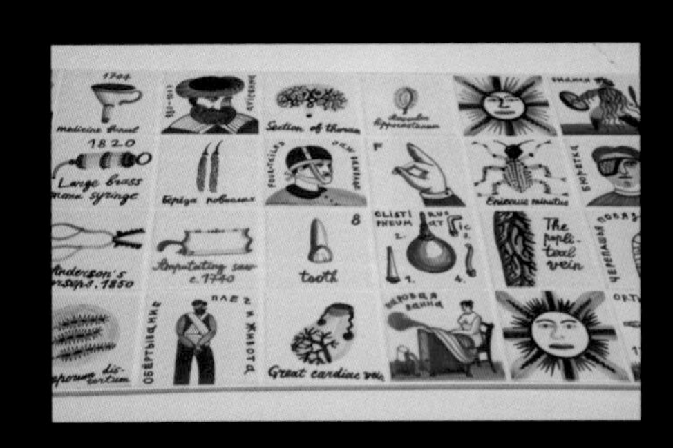

A Brief Medical Encyclopedia
Alexander Florensky, Russian

Actuality #8
Renee Zettle-Sterling, American

Air Show
Lisa Orr, American

Arch
Dmitry Kaminker, Russian

Both Sides of the Brain Puzzlehead Series: A Visual Tribute to Physician Family Members
Dewey Blocksma, American

Burger and Fries
Angela Samuels, American

Clearing II
David Shapiro, American

Cone
Eunmee Lee, Korean

Fortunes of Nature
Harold Linton, American

Four Men Going Fishing,
6a District, Ghana
Dan Watts, American

France Champagne
Pierre Bonnard, French

Function or Submarine
Hoon Lee, Korean

Great Sand Dunes National
Monument, Colorado
David Lubbers, American

GVSU Marching Band
Stuart Padnos, American

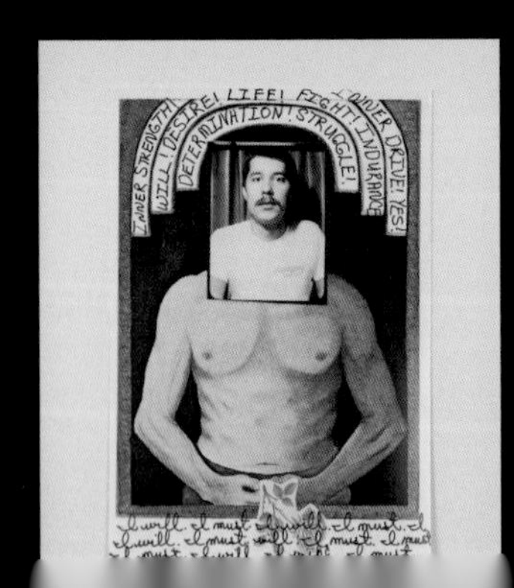

La Catrina y Calavera del Siglo xx
Jose Guadalupe Posada, Mexican

Levels of Knowledge
Ed Wong-Ligda, American

Little Red
John Phillips, American

Luminosity #1, #142, and #149
David Huang, American

Magna Matter
Elona Van Gent, American

Memory
Ann Keister, American

Mundus Imaginalis: Corpus Cognoscendi (Body of Knowledge)
Paul Wittenbraker, American

No Why (Suite)
Dellas Henke, American

Paleolithic Red
Sam Gilliam, American

Pansies
Jo Hormuth, American

Polychrome Acoma Vessel
Robert Patricio, Native American

Reflection of a Hunter Goddess
Tim Fisher, American

Siphonophores
Beverly Seley, American

Studying Drips
Adam Tetzlaff, American

Tablet
Herb Babcock, American

Tall Feats and Long Strides
Carrie Wilson, American

Tao (The Way)
Peimin Ni, Chinese

Untitled
Stephen Duren, American

Untitled
Jill Eggers, American

Untitled
Mark Ripley, American

Village Harmony
Hao Bo Yi, Chinese

Which for Whom?
Steven Sorman, American

Workers in a Field (the Conversation)
Mathias Alten, German-born American

Zonder Titel (Untitled)
Karel Appel, Peirre Alechinsky, Belgia

Additional photos from the 50 favorites are placed throughout this book with a complete index on page 158

DEPARTMENT OF ART AND DESIGN

Since the early years, the Department of Art and Design has enjoyed a growth in enrollment, faculty members and facilities. A major in art was first offered in 1968; in 1976 a bachelor's degree program was added. In between the department had struggled to find appropriate space in the building it shared with the Department of Music. It added the Cedar Studios, built in anticipation of growing enrollments after it received accreditation from the National Association of Schools of Art and Design in 1986.

Another expansion project began in 1996 to consolidate and update teaching facilities for the fine arts. David McGee, then chair of the art department, said it would be the first time that the arts would be together instead of scattered in various buildings. McGee said, "Not only the 220 art majors will benefit, but the one in every 15 Grand Valley students who takes an art class."

In early 1998 a semester-long "Celebration of the Arts" culminated with the dedication of the new art and music facilities. An original Alexander Calder stabile, "Tripes," on loan from the artist's family, was placed in front of the new Calder Art Center. The dedication also included the renovated building that had borne Calder's name since 1969. The former Alexander Calder Fine Arts Center was renamed as the Performing Arts Center. In 1999 the Calder Residence Hall was completed on the southeast end of campus to provide housing for music, art and communication students.

Art Chair David McGee and ceramics instructor Daleene Menning fire raw clay pots outside the new ceramics building, 1996.

In 1998 the new Alexander Calder Art Center (top) was dedicated, and the renovated building that had borne his name since 1969 was renamed the Performing Arts Center (bottom).

Works by an invited group of self-taught artists from Grand Rapids' Heartside area were featured in the 2005 Art Gallery exhibit, 'Raw Art.'

Community outreach has also been a hallmark of Grand Valley's art endeavors, from ceramics students crafting hand-thrown potter's bowls for an annual fundraiser at God's Kitchen, to Civic Studio projects that take the practice of art out of the rarified campus atmosphere and into the gritty reality of an urban community. A 2005 Art Gallery exhibit, "Raw Art," with works by an invited group of self-taught artists from Grand Rapids' Heartside area, broke attendance records from all previous exhibits at Grand Valley. Many of the artists were unemployed and suffered from addictions, mental illness or physical disabilities.

Lubbers continually emphasized the importance of the university's role in the arts community of West Michigan. "At its simplest level, the arts encourage all of us to think creatively," he said. "On a higher level, knowledge of the arts promotes an understanding of our own history and culture, as well as that of other nations."

Grand Valley's first fully endowed chair was created in the art and design department by a gift from the Stuart and Barbara Padnos Foundation. The initial occupant was Steven Sorman, known internationally for his printmaking and painting, who came to Grand Valley in 2008 from Ancram, New York.

ARTS AND HUMANITIES

President Mark A. Murray continued the university's commitment to the arts with the annual Fall Arts Celebration, which began in 2003. His goal was to have a celebration of the many different arts for the enjoyment of the entire campus and the West Michigan community. Since then some of the world's greatest poets, artists, scholars, dancers and musicians have showcased their talents.

Poetry Night has been a popular feature of the celebration, bringing a steady stream of Pulitzer Prize winners to campus. The university's interest in poetry harkens back at least to 1970 when Michigan native Jim Harrison spoke on campus for the first time. Allen Ginsberg made his first visit here as a guest of Thomas Jefferson College for its second National Poetry Festival in 1973. Professor Patricia Clark was named Grand Valley's first Poet-in-Residence during a 1998 celebration to dedicate the new art and music facilities. In 2005 Grand Valley acquired the lifetime papers of Harrison, both a poet and an icon of American literature, for use by researchers and students for generations to come.

Poets Jim Harrison, Galway Kinnell and Dan Gerber are on stage with GVSU Poet-in-Residence Patricia Clark during Poetry Night 2003.

The annual Fall Arts Celebration began in 2003.

Artwork from India's diverse culture was featured during the 2009 Fall Arts Celebration.

Allen Ginsberg (with balloon) sits on steps of the Campus Center during the 1973 National Poetry Festival.

Harrison works with University Archivist Nancy Richard to identify items from more than 300 boxes of his papers, acquired for Grand Valley's Special Collections in 2005.

Celebrating the School of Communications' 20th Anniversary are, left to right, longtime faculty members Barbara Roos, Alex Nesterenko, David Rathbun, Deanna Morse and Roger Ellis, 2003.

Photography, film and video have long held a place in the arts and culture of Grand Valley. These artistic media have provided additional opportunities for interdisciplinary partnerships and guest artists, such as documentary filmmaker Ken Burns and photographer David Plowden.

Barbara Roos, associate professor, founded the film program in the 1970s when it was housed in William James College. She has produced two documentary films that capture some of the university's early history and examine the relationship of liberal to career education.

Films by Professor Deanna Morse, an animation specialist, have been included in permanent collections of the Metropolitan Museum of Art and have aired on "Sesame Street."

Blues on the Banks of the Grand, a benefit concert to raise money for minority scholarships, was established in 1995 by Donald Williams Sr., then dean of the Office of Minority Affairs.

The Summer Film Project has been another opportunity for hands-on learning, with students, faculty and industry professionals joining forces on the production of a short film. In 2007 the project undertook its first feature-length film, "To Live and Die in Dixie," produced and directed by John Harper Philbin, associate professor, who has worked on seven summer films.

Actress Cicely Tyson came to Grand Valley in 2009 to record the narration for the Grand Valley documentary film "Up from the Bottoms: The Search for the American Dream," produced by School of Communications' Adjunct Professor Jim Schaub and his brother Rod Schaub. Another documentary film, "Nightmare in New Guinea," based on the experiences of the Red Arrow soldiers during World War II, was a collaboration of Professor of History James Smither and Frank Boring, an adjunct professor of communications. Both films have been included in the Library of Congress Veterans History Project.

Actress Cicely Tyson records narration for a GVSU documentary about African Americans.

WGVU

On December 17, 1972, WGVC Channel 35, the public television station licensed to Grand Valley's Board of Control, went on the air for the first time. The station was made possible through the financial support of the West Michigan community and a matching grant from the Department of Health, Education and Welfare.

The inaugural program included Lubbers introducing the station to viewers. It was recorded a couple of weeks earlier in the studio of commercial television station WZZM-TV Channel 13, because Grand Valley's 40 x 40-foot studio in the basement of Manitou Hall, in Allendale, was not yet completed. One of the station's first ventures was to inform viewers that the popular "Sesame Street" program would be moving from WZZM to the new local PBS station, WGVC. Invitations were sent to area preschools for an opportunity to meet many of the show's characters at an event in the Fieldhouse at Grand Valley.

As this early logo reflects, the PBS station was launched by Grand Valley State College.

Chuck Furman came to Grand Valley in 1972 and served WGVU for more than 30 years.

Mr. McFeely, a character from 'Mr. Roger's Neighborhood,' visits with young viewers at Grand Valley.

Vice President of University Relations Matt McLogan, right, thanks a challenge grant sponsor at a television pledge drive.

Much of the early programming provided instructional television programs shown in West Michigan classrooms. Each school paid a fee based on the number of students; there were 65,000 young viewers at the start.

Business Television customized programming was beamed via satellite from the station's studios to a variety of businesses, including Meijer and Steelcase.

In one of the first programs locally produced by WGVC, "The People's Business," viewers chose the topic, and people from area organizations came into the studio to share related information and available community services.

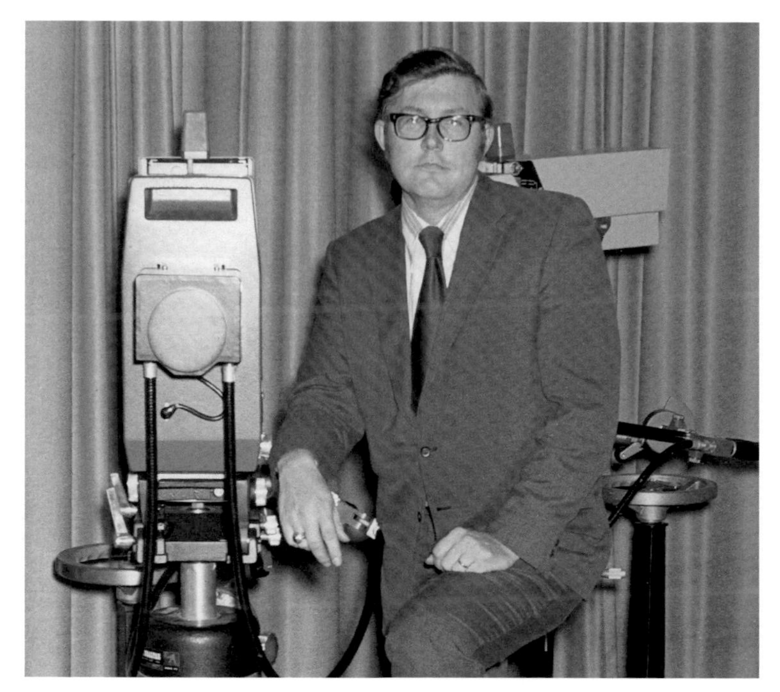

WGVC's first station manager, Gordon Lawrence, poses with the station's first studio cameras.

Michael Walenta, WGVU general manager since 1988, updates the Dream Machine at an auction.

Behind every camera in the studio and on the control boards were students getting relevant, practical application of learned skills. The Arts and Media program in William James College was a forerunner to the current Film and Video Production program in the School of Communications. At the time, a college that had a PBS station was the envy of large universities around the country.

By the 1970s, with the emergence of portable cameras, crews were able to cover more local events. With help from Gerald R. Ford, continuing since his days as a congressman, federal matching funds were acquired to obtain a mobile unit, something that no other station in West Michigan yet had. WGVC was the pioneer station in gavel-to-gavel coverage of political proceedings in Lansing and coverage of many local high school sports.

Grand Valley's radio stations have grown tremendously over the years from the first 25-watt student station. An affiliate of National Public Radio, WGVU-FM 88.5 began broadcasting in 1983 and expanded its power to 3,000 watts in 1987. Audiences grew when WGVU-AM 1480 began simulcast transmissions in 1992. Muskegon's WKBZ AM-FM transferred its license to Grand Valley in 1994, and stations WGVS-AM 850 in Muskegon and WGVS-FM 95.3 in Whitehall went live in 1999. Television coverage extended into Kalamazoo in 1984 when station WGVK-TV, Channel 52, began operation. In 1987 the call letters of Channel 35 were converted to WGVU-TV, reflecting Grand Valley State College's transformation to Grand Valley State University.

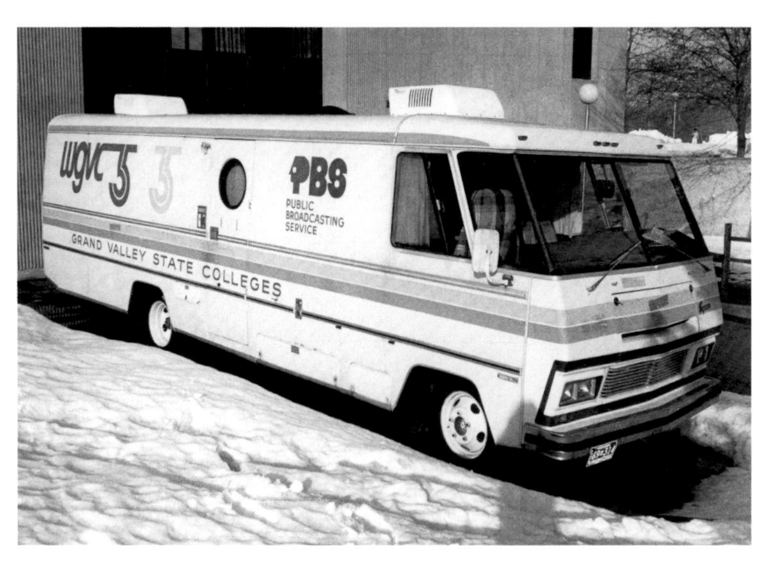

WGVC acquired the first mobile unit in West Michigan in the 1970s with help from federal matching funds.

Ralph and Barb Logerwell, among the hundreds of active volunteers at the station, are shown here at a Great Wine & Food Symposium — an early fundraising event developed for the station; it continues today.

The station's first on-air auction was held in the Fieldhouse in 1975. The auction moved to various locations as it grew larger; it's now held online each spring.

A tremendous growth in facilities began in 1986 as construction got underway for the Grand Rapids Center. Completed in 1988, shortly after Michael Walenta came to Allendale as the third WGVU general manager, it included the new Meijer Public Broadcasting Center.

Much of the non-instructional early programming was community-based. "Michigan Issues and Impact," "Michigan Outdoors" and "The Arts in Michigan" all debuted in the 1990s. The most historic local stories that WGVU covered were Congressman Paul Henry's funeral and the local service following President Ford's death. The station is also the most frequent site for local and state political debates.

Beginning in 2004 the WGVU Digital Campaign to convert the station to digital technology received generous support from public television viewers. The campaign reached its goal of $6.5 million in 2004, with nearly 4,000 individual, corporate and foundation donors providing the needed support.

Prior to the conversion, WGVU-TV reached 1.5 million people. After the conversion, more than 2.7 million viewers received the HD signal, with motion-picture-like quality and access to 5.1 channels of surround sound. With four distinct programming services on three digital channels, the station now offers 63 hours of programming in prime time.

– BY MARY ISCA PIRKOLA

Broadcasting technology has come a long way since this mid-1970s setup in the WGVC-TV studio on the Allendale Campus.

On-air hosts Chris Barbee and Kim Chelsea report highlights from a July 4th celebration in downtown Grand Rapids in the early 1990s.

President Haas, President Emeritus Lubbers, General Manager Michael Walenta and longtime supporter Fred Meijer gather to shut down WGVU's analog television signal, which was replaced by digital technology on June 12, 2009.

GV
421
435
431
46

ATHLETICS

6

DURING THE FIRST YEARS of his presidency, James Zumberge was repeatedly asked the same question: “When is Grand Valley going to have a football team?”

Today, when Laker fans consider the football team’s four national championships, plus national championships in women’s basketball, soccer and volleyball, they often ask Athletic Director Tim Selgo this question: “When is Grand Valley going to move to Division I?”

One thing that is consistent from the early years of Grand Valley's athletic program to its recent successes is the university's commitment to doing what's best for student-athletes. Selgo said it fits with Grand Valley's mission of striving for excellence. "Our programs are achieving success and our student-athletes are students first," he said.

The first sport at Grand Valley was men's cross country, established in 1965 under coach Dave Sharphorn, who was a faculty member in the Physical Education department. Sharphorn would be asked a year later to also coach the men's tennis and basketball teams.

Games and practices during the basketball team's first three years were held at high schools in Allendale, Jenison and Grand Rapids before Grand Valley's Fieldhouse was constructed in 1968. In a *Grand Rapids Press* article Sharphorn recalled those early years: "Obviously, none of the players came to Grand Valley for the expressed purpose of playing basketball. We just sought our own level of competition."

The emphasis for athletics during Grand Valley's early years leaned toward Olympic sports, and there were also early forays into men's golf (1965) and rowing (1966). Rowing remained a varsity sport until 1979 when it switched to club sport status. It remains popular – and successful – today. Team members have raced in England, Croatia, and traditional U.S. regattas in Philadelphia and Tennessee.

Men's cross country was the first sport established at Grand Valley.

Established in 1966, rowing remained a varsity sport until 1979 when it switched to club sport status.

Women's athletics began in 1968. Pictured is a softball player, 1975.

In the late 1960s Grand Valley fans were cheering for the Bruisers, not the Lakers. Team colors were blue, black and white, which led to the unofficial name. Administrators held a contest to name an official mascot and six finalists were selected: Bruisers, Warriors, Bluejays, Ottawas, Archers and Voyagers. Student Annie Kate McDonald, from Grand Haven, came up with a write-in choice: Lakers. After all ballots were counted, Lakers finished 11 votes ahead of Voyagers.

Men's indoor and outdoor track and field started in 1968, and the following year Arend D. Lubbers arrived on campus as Grand Valley's second president. His presidency altered the university's athletic landscape; the most notable change was giving coaches the go-ahead to offer athletic scholarships. "[Lubbers'] appointment as president changed the entire scope of athletics at Grand Valley," Sharphorn told the *Grand Rapids Press*.

Women's athletics started in 1968 after a student asked Joan Boand, a physical education faculty member, to coach softball. Boand said she cajoled Athletic Director Charles Irwin for funds to support softball and, eventually, other women's teams. Within a few years Boand was coaching softball, basketball and volleyball.

FIRST IN MICHIGAN

Grand Valley was the first college in Michigan to award athletic scholarships to women. Joan Boand recruited then offered the first scholarship to softball player Donna Sass Eaton in 1974.

Baseball started in 1968 under coach Hugo Salazar; the Lakers went 1-11 in their first year. Grand Valley's baseball field was completed in 1969, but a heavy winter made the field unplayable, and the team waited until 1970 to play games at its home field.

The fall of 1970 was also the start of Grand Valley's football program, as Robert "Rip" Collins, coach at Grand Rapids' Ottawa Hills High School, was named the first head coach. The team played a junior varsity schedule, preparing for its first varsity year in 1971.

Baseball started in 1968 under coach Hugo Salazar.

Students from Copeland Hall tailgate before a football game, 1987. Arend D. Lubbers saw football as changing Grand Valley from a commuter campus to a residential campus.

Cheerleaders lead the way for the football team.

Women's tennis started in 1971. The team won the 1974 GLIAC tournament under coach Toni Poll.

Pictured is varsity wrestler Phil Cutts during a match in the late-'80s. When it was a varsity sport, wrestling produced 55 All-Americans and eight national champions.

Women's cross country and track and field teams began in the early 1970s.

Lubbers said football changed Grand Valley. "Football gave us the anchor, something you could build your weekend around," he said. The Lakers went winless in their first two football seasons. E. James Harkema was named head coach in 1973.

By 1972 there were 15 sports, including women's tennis, women's cross country and indoor and outdoor track and field (all established in the early '70s).

It didn't take long for the Lakers to establish themselves as a powerhouse within the Great Lakes Intercollegiate Athletic Conference. Women's tennis under coach Toni Poll won the 1974 GLIAC tournament; and men's basketball won the conference championship in 1975 under coach Tom Villemure. The Laker women's basketball team under Boand won the inaugural conference championship in 1975 and continued to win the next four championships. Softball also won five GLIAC championships by 1976.

During the late '70s athletic facilities had to be overhauled and improved. The Fieldhouse dome was condemned in 1978, forcing practices and games to be held elsewhere. Lubbers made it a personal mission to lobby Lansing legislators for state funding for a new athletic facility. Lubbers was instrumental in raising more than $700,000 toward the project's $1 million cost; most of that money came from football fans and private donations.

In recognition of those efforts, Grand Valley's Board of Control named the football stadium and track complex for Lubbers in 1979. A groundbreaking ceremony was held in 1980 on the new $14.5 million athletic complex that would house a swimming pool and basketball arena.

A Christmas tree sits on the dome of the Fieldhouse as a traditional sign of good fortune, 1967. The dome was condemned 10 years later.

Lubbers stands in the press box at Lubbers Stadium, 1988.

GLIAC CHARTER MEMBERS

In 1972 Grand Valley became a charter member of the Great Lakes Intercollegiate Athletic Conference. Other charter members of the now 14-member conference were Ferris State, Lake Superior State, Northwood University and Saginaw Valley State.

Swimmer Anna Polkowski is pictured, 2009. Men's and women's swimming and diving teams started in 1984.

Lubbers' support for athletics led him to the national stage in 1984 when he was named a charter member of the NCAA Presidents Commission. In 1990 he became the first president to be elected to the commission a second time.

Men's and women's swimming and diving teams were established in 1984 under head coach Dewey Newsome. Newsome remained head coach for 23 years.

In 1989, under head coach Tom Beck, the Laker football team posted its first undefeated season at 11-0 and finished third in the final NCAA Division II poll. Also that year the GLIAC dropped football as a conference sport. Grand Valley and the other conference members joined the Heartland Collegiate Conference to form the Midwest Intercollegiate Football Conference; league play began in 1990.

Apparently it didn't matter which conference Grand Valley played in, as the Lakers won the first MIFC title. The MIFC continued until 1999, when league members merged with the GLIAC.

Two coaches were hired in 1991, and both – Brian Kelly (football) and Doug Woods (softball) – would see great successes in their sports. Kelly had been a Grand Valley assistant coach, and Woods served as Grand Valley's athletic trainer and a faculty member in the Movement Science department.

Lubbers saw an opportunity to heighten Grand Valley's athletic facilities in the early 1990s when he led an advisory committee through the process of building a golf course on campus. Because it was important to enhance the Allendale Campus' wetlands, the committee, which included biology and geology faculty members, chose environmentally conscious Michael Hurdzan as course architect.

The Meadows opened in 1994 after special attention was paid to wetlands preservation.

The Lakers play the Saginaw Valley Cardinals in the Fieldhouse, 1985. That year Grand Valley made its first appearance in the NCAA tournament and advanced to the second round before losing to South Dakota State.

Once a version of a character from *The Old Man and the Sea*, the Laker mascot got a makeover in 1996. Louie the Laker is now one of Grand Valley's most visible identities.

The Meadows opened in 1994. The complex includes a practice facility and clubhouse. Since opening, it has hosted six NCAA national golf championships, with a seventh set for 2011. *Links Magazine* ranked it among the top 25 college golf courses in the country.

To comply with Title IX legislation, wrestling switched from varsity to club sport status in the 1990s. It continues to be a popular club sport for Grand Valley students. Team members have won five National Collegiate Wrestling Association championships since 2001.

In 1996 women's soccer was added and Dago Cortes was named first head coach. Also that year the Laker mascot received a makeover. The Lakers had been represented by "the Great Laker," a version of a character from *The Old Man and the Sea*. Selgo and Marketing Director Rob Odejewski named the mascot "Louie" and worked to brand the character. Since Louie's inception, his character has gone through minor revisions but remains one of Grand Valley's most visible identities.

Selgo increased the number of scholarships for women's golf and hired its first full-time coach, Lori Stinson, in 1999. That same year Jerry Baltes was hired to coach men's and women's track and cross country programs. Baltes quickly made the Lakers a conference powerhouse and national contender as the women's cross country team placed fifth at the NCAA national championships that year.

During the first 10 years that Baltes led Grand Valley's programs, the Lakers won 48 out of 54 possible GLIAC championships in cross country, and indoor and outdoor track and field. Many of Baltes' student-athletes have won individual NCAA titles, including distance runner and eight-time NCAA top medalist Mandi Zemba.

In 2001 the Laker volleyball team advanced to its first NCAA final four tournament. The Lakers, under coach Deanne Scanlon, also made final four appearances in 2002 and 2003.

Softball won the Great Lakes Regional Tournament in 2002 and advanced to the national championships. A year later Woods won his 500th game.

Nate Miller clears the high jump bar, 2009.

The Laker volleyball team made its first appearance in the NCAA tournament in 2001 and won the championship in 2005.

Curt Anes won the Harlon Hill Award as the nation's best Division II player and led the Lakers to their first national football title in 2002.

The Lakers have appeared in six national championship games in nine years and won national titles in 2002, 2003, 2005 and 2006.

Permanent lights were added to Lubbers Stadium before the start of the 2001 football season. Night games and success led to increased crowds. In 2009 at a game against Saginaw State, Laker fans set a GVSU attendance record at 16,467. The addition of live Webcasts of games in 2002 and the Grand Valley Sports Network gave Laker fans across the country more opportunities to follow their team.

The football team posted a 10-0 regular season record in 2001 and advanced to the national championship in Florence, Alabama, before losing to North Dakota, 17-14, in the game's last minutes. "Finish What We Started" was the team motto a year later, and the mantra worked. Led by quarterback Curt Anes and wide receiver David Kircus, the Lakers beat Valdosta State. Kelly brought the Lakers back to Alabama for the championship game in 2003, and the team beat North Dakota, 10-3, to win back-to-back national football championships.

Mark A. Murray talks with former Detroit Lions coach Steve Mariucci at the Fieldhouse.

The 2005 Laker volleyball team is pictured after winning the national championship in Kearney, Nebraska.

The Lakers play in the 2004 College World Series championship game against Delta State but lose, 12-8.

Evan Betts dives in the Fieldhouse pool, 2008.

Lori Andjelich throws a pitch during a game against Ferris State, 2007.

Golfer Melissa Sneller won Grand Valley's first individual golf national championship in 2005. Sneller and a Florida Southern golfer were tied after four rounds in Albuquerque, New Mexico, when Sneller sank a five-foot birdie on the 18th hole to win.

Other teams also saw success in 2003. The women's golf team finished fifth at the NCAA Division II national tournament. For the first time, Laker baseball and coach Steve Lyon advanced to the College World Series.

Successes in 2003-2004 led to the university winning its first Directors' Cup trophy, presented by the National Association of Collegiate Directors of America to the college or university with the best all-sports program in the country. That year began a streak of six consecutive Directors' Cup wins for Grand Valley. The streak is concurrent with the GLIAC Presidents' Cup Trophy, presented to the top athletic program in the conference; GVSU has won that honor the past 11 years in a row.

In 2004 Chuck Martin, former Laker defensive coordinator, was named head coach. Martin coached two teams that won national football championships. He left Grand Valley in 2009 to serve as defensive backs coach under Kelly at Notre Dame. Matt Mitchell, who was the Lakers' defensive coordinator, was named head coach in January 2010.

Volleyball continued to be a powerhouse in 2005, advancing to the national championships in Kearney, Nebraska. Before a record Division II volleyball crowd of more than 5,000, Grand Valley beat host Nebraska-Kearney, 3-1, to win the university's first national title in a women's sport.

The 2006 Laker basketball team lost only one game that season and won the national title, beating American International College, 58-52.

NCAA President Myles Brand (with microphone) presents the Directors' Cup to Grand Valley, 2008.

Football took a 9-0 record into postseason play in 2005 (the last game of the regular season was canceled because of lightning). The Lakers advanced to the Division II championship game, their fourth appearance in five years, and beat Northwest Missouri State, 21-17, to win their third national championship.

The women's basketball team, under coach Dawn Plitzuweit, won its first national championship in 2006. The team lost only one game that year and beat American International College, 58-52, for the national crown.

The soccer team and coach Dave DiIanni advanced to the national championship game in 2006 but lost a 1-0 heartbreaker to Metro State. In 2009 the soccer team beat Cal State Dominguez Hills, 1-0, to win the national championship. GVSU finished that year undefeated at 22-0-4.

Football again advanced to the national championship game in 2006, bringing a 14-0 record to Florence, Alabama, where the Lakers captured their fourth title with a 17-14 win over Northwest Missouri State.

In 2007 men's basketball made the first of two straight trips to the NCAA Elite Eight under coach Ric Wesley. The athletic program expanded in 2009 when it was announced that women's lacrosse would be added as a varsity sport.

Throughout its 50-year history, a mainstay of Laker athletics has been to ensure that student-athletes are students first. The Laker Academic Advising Center provides academic support to Grand Valley's 500 student-athletes.

Callistus Eziukwu beats a University of Michigan defender, 2006. The 6-foot 6-inch center went on to play professional basketball in Europe.

The soccer team celebrates its national title in 2009 after beating Cal State Dominguez Hills, 1-0.

Throughout its 50-year history, a mainstay of Laker athletics has been to ensure that student-athletes are students first. The Laker Academic Advising Center provides academic support to Grand Valley's 500 student-athletes. Countless student-athletes have been named to Academic All-America teams. Notably in 2008 soccer's Katy Tafler received the prestigious NCAA Top VIII Award, as one of eight outstanding student-athletes selected for their academic achievement, athletic success and community service.

Each Laker team participates in regular community service projects. In 2007 a third of the football team traveled to Mississippi to help build homes for Hurricane Katrina victims still struggling from the 2005 disaster.

Katy Tafler received the NCAA Top VIII Award, given to the nation's outstanding student-athletes.

Blake Smolen breaks away from a University of Findlay tackle. The Lakers again made a road trip to Florence, Alabama, for the championship game in 2009 but lost to Northwest Missouri State, 30-23.

Laker fans dress for the occasion in Lubbers Stadium, 2008.

The volunteer efforts, academic success and athletic accomplishments create a solid sports program that is recognized nationally. "We've found our niche in college athletics and will continue to try to be the best program in Division II," Selgo said.

– BY MICHELE COFFILL

THE FUTURE OF MANKIND
John Adams
The Archaeologist At Work
KIPLING
STUDENT SERVICES BUILDING

CAMPUS GROWTH

7

WHILE IT WOULDN'T BE ACCURATE TO SAY there was nothing in Allendale before Grand Valley, it would have been hard to imagine the way a swath of pastoral farmland south of M-45 would be transformed into the densely packed university of today.

Grand Valley's future home was selected by a committee from a series of proposals that included several West Michigan sites, said Grand Valley founder L. William Seidman. "There were some bitter arguments about whether or not it shouldn't be closer to or in downtown Grand Rapids, whether it shouldn't be closer to Holland or Muskegon. But we eventually got a place that was centrally located but close enough to Grand Rapids so that people could commute there," Seidman said.

By 1962 there was plenty of action in Allendale. Construction of the first academic buildings was underway, but administration and an early version of a library were handled out of a pair of homes on M-45: a two-story structure dubbed the Grey House and a one-story ranch next door called the Pink House (pictured on page 35).

Future Provost Glenn A. Niemeyer interviewed for a faculty position in the Grey House in early 1963. "I came there and was ushered to the second floor in what had been a bedroom, and as I was being interviewed, it was difficult to get beyond the fact that this had once been a bedroom rather than an office," he said.

Classes began at the end of September 1963. The first buildings in the Great Lakes Group – Lake Michigan Hall and Lake Superior Hall – were still under construction.

Located on M-45, the Grey House serves as the first administration building.

The arches used during construction in Grand Valley's early years continue as an architectural theme today.

"Lake Michigan Hall was not finished by the time we were expected to begin in the fall," Niemeyer said. "The first day, there were no parking lots that were paved. All of the ground around there was clay and it had been unusually wet, and so everybody was tromping through this clay, and by the time we got to the building our shoes were just covered with mud."

Niemeyer continued: "Lake Michigan Hall is a square turned on a square, which is a very difficult building to navigate, to know exactly where you are; and you were going around and around in this building and only recalled that you had missed wherever you should be when you rounded it the second time."

Pictured is construction of Lake Michigan Hall, the university's first building.

In 1965 the Great Lakes group of buildings was named 'Building of the Month' by *College and University Business* magazine.

Loutit Hall of Science opened in 1966.

A journeyman bricklayer named John Scherff came to work at Grand Valley as a groundskeeper in 1964. He described an environment of gravel parking lots and "no grounds to speak of whatsoever."

"I spent my first winter pulling a good number of people out with the tractor because the gravel got wet, and of course people got stuck," Scherff remembered.

Through the '60s the young institution experienced its first growth spurt, setting the ground for many features that are familiar to Grand Valley students today. Seidman House opened in 1964 as a student center, bookstore, recreation room and offices for student groups. Lake Huron Hall also opened that year. Loutit Hall of Science opened in 1966.

The Little Mac Bridge was erected in 1965. The 230-foot pedestrian bridge spans a 70-foot-deep ravine and connects the north and south ends of campus.

Allendale began making its first steps toward becoming a residential campus in 1966 with the opening of James M. Copeland House. That building was joined by Kenneth W. Robinson House in 1967 and Grace Olsen Kistler House in 1971. The three buildings were named for founding members of the Board of Control. All of the S-shaped buildings in this housing complex curving along the ravine are now called living centers. They were renovated in the 2000s.

"We thought, to begin with, we would be a commuting campus because people would have no place to stay until we could build something," Seidman said. "But we had in mind always that it would become a residential campus and that ... living on the campus would give the students an experience that would be very worthwhile."

Grand Valley's first student housing consisted of three S-shaped buildings along the ravine.

Constructing a living center.

Built in 1966 Copeland Living Center opened as the first student housing on campus.

A familiar sight to anyone who has lived on campus, The Commons dining facility was completed in 1968.

The next step in the growth of the Allendale Campus began in 1967 with construction of Mackinac Hall, the first in a new group of buildings known as the Islands Complex. It was followed by Manitou Hall in 1968.

The year 1968 saw continued growth, but also an ill omen. During construction, the center section of the Fieldhouse – commonly known as the Dome – collapsed in February. The building opened in time for graduation in 1969 but stayed open for less than a decade. In 1978 the Dome was closed again due to water damage and danger of the roof collapsing. In 1979 Grand Valley took legal action against the architects for failing to meet acceptable design requirements. The Dome was demolished in January 1980 and replaced by the current Fieldhouse.

Students gather outside The Commons.

The ill-fated Dome was demolished in 1980 and replaced by the current Fieldhouse.

Named for Grand Valley's first president, the James H. Zumberge Library was completed in 1969.

Workers construct the Ravines.

With the changing of the guard in 1969 from President Zumberge to President Arend D. Lubbers, the James H. Zumberge Library was dedicated. It earned an award from *College and University Business* magazine for the library's imaginative approach to college building design and an Honor Award for architectural excellence from the Michigan Society of Architects.

The site of countless concerts, plays and other events, the 500-seat Louis Armstrong Theatre opened in 1971 as part of the Calder Fine Arts building (later renamed the Performing Arts Center).

Grand Valley was on the cutting-edge again in 1973 with the opening of the Ravines Apartments. It was the first on-campus townhouse-style student apartment development in Michigan and one of few in the nation.

Opened in 1973 the Ravines was the first on-campus townhouse development in Michigan.

The Board of Control voted in 1979 to pay tribute to President Lubbers by naming the new football stadium after him. "I don't know what to say," said a surprised Lubbers after the vote, "so I'll say nothing. Thank you very much."

Coming out of the painful dissolution of the cluster college system at Grand Valley, the institution turned its sights a dozen miles to the east, to downtown Grand Rapids. Michigan was deep in a recession in the early 1980s, and Lubbers' decision to expand into Grand Rapids was controversial.

The new Fieldhouse was completed in 1982. The athletic complex has been expanded and now features a state-of-the-art fitness center.

Construction crews work at the newly named Arend D. Lubbers Stadium in 1979.

Arend D. Lubbers speaks at the groundbreaking ceremony for what would become the L.V. Eberhard Center, 1986.

"We had a market in Grand Rapids," Lubbers said. "To come to Grand Rapids would be a great convenience for the students we had. That was justification for coming here and for building here in the city." Lubbers added that building a high-profile campus in downtown Grand Rapids would increase Grand Valley's visibility, and it would help with the redevelopment of the city's West Side.

Internally, Lubbers said some were concerned that Allendale would be neglected or abandoned with the construction of a Grand Rapids campus. His response: "Allendale will be helped by this, and it's going to be helped because of the presence. I think there was a considerable amount of skepticism about that. But I believe I've been proven right about it." Ground was broken for the L.V. Eberhard Center in 1986, and the building opened in 1988.

WGVU graphic designers work on Macs and typesetting machines in Eberhard Center, 1988.

Opened in 1988, the Eberhard Center houses Grand Valley's College of Education, WGVU radio and television studios, Pew Campus Security and Conference Services.

Opened in 1995 the Student Services Building is home to Admissions, Financial Aid, Records and Registration, Housing, Career Services, Counseling Center and the Dean of Students Office.

Grand Valley continued to add housing in Allendale, opening Hoobler, Weed, Ott and Johnson living centers in 1987 and Pickard, DeVos and Pew living centers in 1989.

In 1991 the Cook-DeWitt Center opened with a 250-seat auditorium and offices for Campus Ministry. The building was named for Peter and Pat Cook and Marvin and Jerene DeWitt. Paul B. Henry Hall and Student Services opened in 1995, and Seymour & Esther Padnos Hall of Science opened in 1996.

In 1986 Grand Valley's enrollment was 8,361. By 2004 it had soared to 22,063. Bob Fletcher was given much of the credit for that growth as well as for Grand Valley's embrace of cutting-edge technology.

Fletcher spent 25 years lending his energy, leadership and insight to the university as associate director of admissions, dean of academic services and later vice provost and dean of academic services, overseeing admissions, information technology and financial aid.

"There was no better mind in the fields of admissions and computers than Bob's," said Lubbers. "His contributions to develop and manage the growth of Grand Valley are something people outside of the university wouldn't see or attribute to him." Lynn (Chick) Blue now serves in this role and continues to lead technological advances at Grand Valley.

With Allendale growing quickly, it was time for the university to turn its sights back to Grand Rapids. Grand Valley broke ground in 1997 for a $50 million Grand Rapids campus expansion.

Crews work to build the Student Services Building; in the foreground is the Cook-DeWitt Center.

Many construction projects in the mid-'90s changed the look of the Allendale Campus.

The Richard M. DeVos Center — with its distinctive Beckering Family Carillon tower — opened in 2000.

The new building was named for Amway co-founder Richard M. DeVos and further raised Grand Valley's profile downtown. In 2000 the campus was named for Robert C. Pew, recognizing his leadership on the Board of Control and his role in expanding Grand Valley's presence in Grand Rapids.

"Buildings are symbolic as well as functional," Lubbers said. "The DeVos Center makes a major statement about our commitment to downtown Grand Rapids. Its architecture and interior design sets a high standard of quality, and, I believe, alerts the citizens of the state that Grand Valley is a university striving to be the best."

Nancy Lubbers stands with her children, Andy and Caroline, during the dedication of the Nancy Lubbers Garden in the DeVos Center, 2000.

The 1990s was a period of explosive enrollment growth at Grand Valley. One result of that growth was an increasing base of alumni. In 2000 the Alumni House and Visitor Center opened its doors.

"It was a grand addition to the campus, it made a statement," said retired Alumni Relations Director Nancee Miller. "It says that this university graduates students who love Grand Valley and who have invested in it and are willing to continue their investment in it. It also says something about Grand Valley's pride in its graduates, and that there's a supportive relationship between the two entities."

In 2001 ground was broken for the Cook-DeVos Center for Health Sciences on the corner of Michigan and Lafayette in Grand Rapids – in the heart of an area now known as "Medical Mile" that features Spectrum Health, Van Andel Institute, and the Michigan State University College of Human Medicine, among others. The building, filled with state-of-the-art labs and beautiful original artwork, opened in 2003.

"In the beginning, I suppose, there were some people who thought that Grand Valley erecting a building on the Medical Mile was a kind of planting of the flag and expressing, 'We're here and we want to be a part of this,'" said Ron VanSteeland, retired vice president for Finance and Administration. "But it's so much more than that in terms of its ultimate importance to the viability of the medical community in Grand Rapids because we are very much a part of that team."

James Moyer, assistant vice president for Facilities Planning, signs a wall during construction of a parking garage on the Robert C. Pew Grand Rapids Campus, 2004. Moyer is responsible for planning campus growth and ensuring the university's commitment to sustainability.

Solidifying Grand Valley's hold on engineering education in Grand Rapids, the Seymour and Esther Padnos College of Engineering and Computing's Keller Engineering Laboratories opened next to the Eberhard Center in 2000, and the John C. Kennedy Hall of Engineering opened adjacent to that in 2007.

The Cook-DeVos Center for Health Sciences expands Grand Valley's connection to Grand Rapids' 'Medical Mile.'

In its next phase of growth, Grand Valley established a strong commitment to environmental sustainability in its facilities. When the Michigan Alternative and Renewable Energy Center in Muskegon opened in 2003, it was considered a cutting-edge leader in green technology. It was Grand Valley's first building to receive the coveted LEED certification from the U.S. Green Building Council. LEED stands for Leadership in Energy and Environmental Design and is an internationally recognized certification system that certifies environmentally sustainable construction projects. By 2009 the university had 15 structures that have been either LEED-certified or are in various stages of being certified, offering visible signs of Grand Valley's commitment to making its operations more environmentally responsible.

"We have now begun to look at the buildings themselves, to make sure they are as environmentally friendly as we can get them," said James Moyer, assistant vice president for Facilities Planning. "We've got people asking some fundamental questions: not 'Is that right or wrong?' but 'Can we sustain our current way of life?'"

The Glenn A. Niemeyer Learning and Living Center carries a LEED Silver designation. Serving as home to the Frederik Meijer Honors College, it has classroom space and housing for 450 students. Jeff Chamberlain, director of the Honors College, called it "an optimal environment for student living and learning, a place that nurtures a genuine academic community."

Jim Bachmeier, vice president for Finance and Administration, addresses a question during a Board of Trustees meeting. Bachmeier was appointed vice president in 2006 and has managed the financing for most of Grand Valley's LEED-certified projects.

Lake Ontario Hall is the fifth member of the Great Lakes group of buildings. Opened in 2005, it was the first LEED-certified building on the Allendale Campus.

Pictured is the green roof on the Kennedy Hall of Engineering.

Mackinac Hall underwent expansion in 2008. Pictured in front is Cyril Lixenberg's 'Amaranth,' one of the top 50 favorite pieces of art from the university's collections.

As Grand Valley looks to the future, the university's No. 1 priority is a replacement for Zumberge Library. That facility is at the center of Grand Valley's "Shaping Our Future" campaign – the university's first-ever comprehensive campaign. The proposed Mary Idema Pew Library Learning and Information Commons will use new technology and structural design to facilitate education for the 21st century.

"Our top priority continues to be a new library, but this will not be the kind of library most of us are used to," said President Thomas J. Haas. "We need to replace the library that was built in Allendale to serve a couple thousand students with a new kind of library for the information age. It will serve our 24,000 students who are looking for the tools they'll need to build their own futures and contribute to the overall economy of the region."

– BY BRIAN J. BOWE

SUCCESS STORIES

8

THE FIRST 50 YEARS AT GRAND VALLEY were decades of tremendous growth. What will the next 50 years bring? We think the answer is still tremendous growth, but not in terms of numbers of buildings or students.

It's the people of Grand Valley – students, alumni, faculty and staff members – who will help shape the university as it enters its next decades. Here are snapshots of a few people who are making a positive impact in their communities. Enjoy these stories as a representation, not a complete listing, of the notable and innovative contributions Lakers are making in their communities and around the world.

Jennifer Haberling was named Michigan's Teacher of the Year. Her students at Baldwin Street Middle School think she's tops, too.

JENNIFER HABERLING, TEACHER

Little did she know that being Michigan's Teacher of the Year came with so many responsibilities. In May 2008 Jennifer Haberling, '94, was surprised with the announcement that she was selected to represent the state's top teachers.

She spent a whirlwind year traveling around Michigan and the U.S., meeting educators, legislators, parents and students, trying to soak up as much information as possible to bring back to her English classroom at Baldwin Street Middle School in Hudsonville.

"I've been so fortunate to meet all these people and pick their brains about best practices in education and also to share some of our successes in West Michigan," Haberling said. Among her duties as Teacher of the Year, Haberling was a non-voting member at State Board of Education meetings, and she got to attend Space Camp in Huntsville, Alabama.

A career diplomat, John Beyrle credits Grand Valley for teaching him to explore the world. He received the Distinguished Alumnus Award in 2010.

JOHN BEYRLE, U.S. AMBASSADOR

As U.S. Ambassador to Russia, John Beyrle, '75, is on the frontlines of building solid, productive relations between the two countries. After attending meetings with President Barack Obama and Russian President Dmitry Medvedev, Beyrle said the two presidents seem to have similar goals.

"This is a rare moment in our relationship, a moment full of possibilities," Beyrle told area audiences during visits in 2009.

The U.S. Senate confirmed Beyrle as ambassador in 2008. He credits his Grand Valley professors for pushing him to explore the world. "It just opened a huge door to the outside world to me. I went through that door and I've been traveling ever since," he said.

Jermale Eddie serves a church congregation and college students in Texas.

JERMALE EDDIE, YOUTH MINISTRY DIRECTOR

Jermale Eddie, '99, said goodbye to Grand Rapids and a comfortable life in 2008 and drove his wife to Port Arthur, Texas, to help start a church there with his friend and mentor. He was immediately welcomed by hurricanes Gustav and Ike within a month of arriving.

After two mandatory evacuations, Eddie stuck with his plan. "We knew from the very beginning that God purposed us here to start Impact United Methodist Church so we can make a positive influence on the community," he said.

Impact UMC, where Eddie serves as director of student ministries, continues to grow its congregation. Eddie is also the assistant director of student activities at Lamar University in Beaumont, Texas.

DEBORAH CLANTON, MAGISTRATE

As a magistrate and director of probation services, Deborah Clanton, '76, has moments when she wishes today's parents acted more like her mom. Shirley Griffin had other ideas when her daughter said she was going to leave Grand Valley because she couldn't decide on a career.

"I called home to tell my mother I was quitting school, and she took it upon herself to call Dean Earl Harper, who got me registered into three different career paths," Clanton said. Through a criminal justice class, Clanton found a passion for that field and worked as a corrections officer and counselor in a women's prison before beginning a 25-year career in a Kentwood courtroom.

While at Grand Valley, Clanton was a charter member of Delta Sigma Theta Sorority. She remains involved in the national sorority's initiatives. She received the Distinguished Alumna Award in 2008. "I'm so thankful to my mom for not letting me quit school," Clanton said.

LOUISA STARK, GENETICIST

Louisa Stark, '79, is a leader in genetics and genomics education. Now the director of the University of Utah's Genetic Science Learning Center, Stark credits her years as a teaching assistant at Grand Valley as providing the foundation to pursue a career as a science educator. Stark received the Distinguished Alumna Award in 2009 and a prestigious award from the journal *Science* for best online resources in education.

Magistrate Deborah Clanton, in her Kentwood courtroom, was a charter member of Grand Valley's Delta Sigma Theta sorority.

MUSICIANS EARN CRITICAL ACCLAIM

Not content to rest on their 2009 performance at Carnegie Hall, members of Grand Valley's New Music Ensemble continue to earn national attention, and – more importantly – bring modern classical music to a wider audience.

Founded in 2006 by director Bill Ryan, the NME is comprised of stellar student, faculty and community musicians. They quickly gained popularity in 2007 after a 5 a.m. performance of Steve Reich's "Music for 18 Musicians" at the Bang On a Can Marathon in New York City. That was followed by a critically acclaimed CD release of the composition. In addition to making numerous "Best Of" lists (*New York Times, LA Weekly, Washington Post, New York Magazine*), the recording spent 11 weeks on the *Billboard* classical charts.

NME members were invited in 2009 to perform with the Kronos Quartet and others at Carnegie Hall in celebration of the 45th anniversary of Terry Riley's "In C." Ryan said despite preparing for that performance for an entire year, ensemble members were a bit nervous about playing for Riley and other world-class musicians. "Very soon we realized that they were all very nice and welcoming," Ryan said.

NME released its second CD in 2009; it's an NME recording of "In C," which Ryan then sent to top re-mixers around the country to create their own mixes. The two-CD set bridges diverse genres like techno, electronica, dance, pop, jazz and modern classical.

Bill Ryan conducts the New Music Ensemble during a performance at Carnegie Hall.

DAVID ROBINSON, SINGER

David Robinson brought the crowd to its feet at the 2009 Convocation when he performed a stirring rendition of "The Impossible Dream" from the musical "Man of La Mancha." He also sang "What a Wonderful World" at the memorial service for Grand Valley founder L. William Seidman and during a Fall Arts Celebration event. Yet Robinson surprises even his friends when they find out his major is not music but advertising and public relations.

Robinson is an accomplished baritone who has performed with several Grand Valley ensembles and the gospel choir, Voices of GVSU. He started at Grand Valley as a music student and said he is thankful for keeping his ties with music faculty members, even after switching his major.

"You always hear about starving actors," he said. "Hopefully, I'll be one who's not starving but going to auditions while working at a good job in a public relations firm."

AWARD-WINNING MUSICIAN

Troy Hardy, '95, is a well-known music editor, composer and guitarist in Los Angeles. He has worked as a music editor on more than 250 television shows, including "Entourage," "CSI" and "Grey's Anatomy."

He has received four Emmy Award nominations and earned Motion Picture Sound Editors Golden Reel nominations for Best Sound Editing. Hardy received Grand Valley's Distinguished Alumnus Award in 2009.

Baritone David Robinson sings during the memorial service for L. William Seidman.

Bringing world-class speakers to Grand Rapids is part of Dixie Anderson's job at the World Affairs Council of Western Michigan.

DIXIE ANDERSON, WORLD AFFAIRS COUNCIL EXECUTIVE

Dixie Anderson, '72 and '78, has brought the world to Grand Rapids in her role as executive director of the World Affairs Council of Western Michigan. The council's mission is to educate people about foreign policy issues that are facing the nation.

Through Anderson's efforts, the council has hosted such diverse guest speakers as South African Archbishop Desmond Tutu, former President George W. Bush, author Tom Friedman and former Pakistan President Pervez Musharraf. "We really work for a good mix of speakers from all sides of the political spectrum," Anderson said. "The council believes our mission is to stimulate discussion about various foreign policy issues, not to tell people what to think."

The WAC national office named the Western Michigan council "Best Small Council in the Nation" in 2002. Anderson was among the first women to complete a master's of business administration degree at Grand Valley. She helped establish the Seidman College of Business Alumni Association; Anderson earned the Alumni Service Award in 1991 and the Distinguished Alumna Award in 2005.

JONATHAN WHITE, LIBERAL STUDIES CHAIR

After a distinguished career in criminal justice, including a stint as a world-renowned expert in religious terrorism, Professor Jonathan White has found a new niche as chair of Grand Valley's Liberal Studies Department.

"I've found that liberal studies students are eclectic, multi-disciplinary and dedicated to the pursuit of learning," he said. The same can be said about White.

Following the September 11 terrorist attacks, White was tapped by the U.S. Department of Justice to increase his role in anti-terrorism training with police agencies throughout the world.

White helped establish Grand Valley's School of Criminal Justice in the early 1980s and served as dean of social sciences. He is an ordained Christian pastor and a former SWAT team member. Now, after nearly four years of government travel, he's content to be again at the front of the classroom.

"I have absolutely found a home in Liberal Studies. I spent the summer re-reading Plato, Aristotle, and all the books I had read as a undergraduate history major," White said. "It's so wonderful to get to the richness of liberal studies. And I laughed a lot while reading Plato; he's quite humorous."

Now at home again in a classroom, Jonathan White worked for the federal government conducting anti-terrorism training for police agencies after the September 11 attacks.

PROFESSORS REACH OUT TO COMMUNITY

Professor Shirley Fleischmann incorporates community service into her engineering courses. Students in Fleischmann's classes have helped build an energy-efficient house for a low-income family, repaired bicycles for an elementary school class and designed a playroom for a nonprofit agency. John Kilbourne, professor of movement science, brings together sustainability and fitness with a project in which young students pedal an exercise bicycle that produces usable electrical energy.

Research by nursing professor Linda Scott and others has influenced how some hospitals monitor and set staffing hours for nurses.

LINDA SCOTT, PROFESSOR AND RESEARCHER

Linda Scott, '95, set a goal for herself when she graduated from high school: to someday "make just a bit of difference." As professor of nursing in the Kirkhof College of Nursing, the difference Scott has made has influenced how some hospitals set staffing hours for nurses.

Scott and a colleague from the University of Pennsylvania have researched staff nurse fatigue, or how the number of continuous hours a staff nurse works may affect patient safety. Their research has proven to be an evidential base that policy-makers turn to when making recommendations for patient safety and staff work hours.

In 2008 Scott was inducted into the American Academy of Nurses. Academy fellows are nursing's most accomplished practitioners, educators and researchers. In 2009, she was named a faculty recipient of a Niemeyer Award, named in honor of former Provost Glenn A. Niemeyer.

"When I entered college," Scott said, "I had a goal of pursuing a rigorous science-based discipline. Being able to make a difference for patients and for students has given me the opportunity to have the best of both worlds."

ALAN STEINMAN, AWRI DIRECTOR

Alan Steinman, director of the Annis Water Resources Institute, continues to be an environmental champion and advocate for the Great Lakes and its inland waters.

Established in 1986, the AWRI has been committed to the study of freshwater resources through public education, research and outreach. Steinman has led its operations since 2001. He is a national expert who serves on a science advisory board for the Environmental Protection Agency, assists with the International Joint Commission's water level study in the Great Lakes and has served on state groundwater and phosphorus advisory councils.

A career ecologist who has testified before Congress on water resources, Steinman said he's cautiously optimistic about the state of the environment and its future. "The major bottleneck is that it is really hard to get people to change their behavior," he said, referring to small and large steps, like not using fertilizers with phosphorus on lawns and adopting new regulations to limit carbon dioxide emissions.

He added that future environmental efforts will best come from a multidisciplinary approach. "Science continues to improve, but science only informs policy, it does not dictate it," Steinman said. "It's critical that we tackle these problems not only as ecologists but also with economists and sociologists at our side to help ensure that we protect our planet's natural resources."

Alan Steinman, shown at a storm water tank, and researchers at the Annis Water Resources Institute are passionate advocates for the Great Lakes and its inland waters.

1960
50
2010
Years of Shaping Lives
GRAND VALLEY
STATE UNIVERSITY

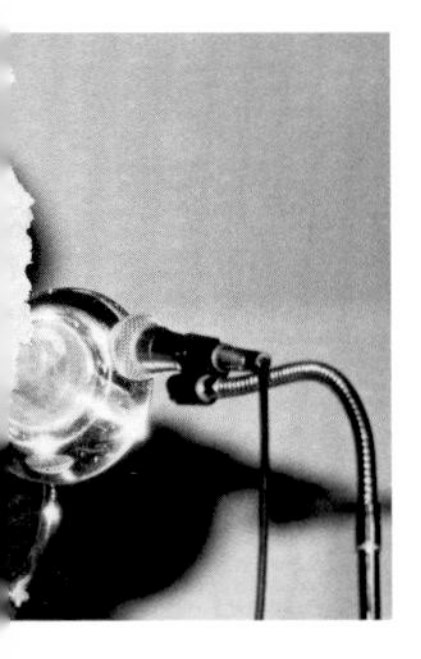

1972 Five cluster colleges form; name changes to Grand Valley State Colleges.

1982 The cluster colleges disband. Reorganization moves toward professional schools.

1979 Board of Control names football stadium after Lubbers.

1971 Calder Fine Arts Center opens, creating a permanent home for student and faculty performances.

1986 First Presidents' Ball draws 300 people to the Kirkhof Center. Now the event brings more than 4,000 to Grand Rapids venues to dance the night away.

1980s

1972 WGVC Channel 35 goes live. Since that time, Grand Valley has been committed to maintaining public broadcast radio and television stations.

1977 First foreign university partnership is established in Krakow, Poland.

1985 Grand Valley celebrates its silver anniversary.

THE FIRST 50 YEARS

1960 Michigan Legislature establishes Grand Valley State College; West Michigan committee, led by L. William Seidman, selects Allendale and purchases land.

1964 Seidman House opens as a student center, bookstore and home of music performances.

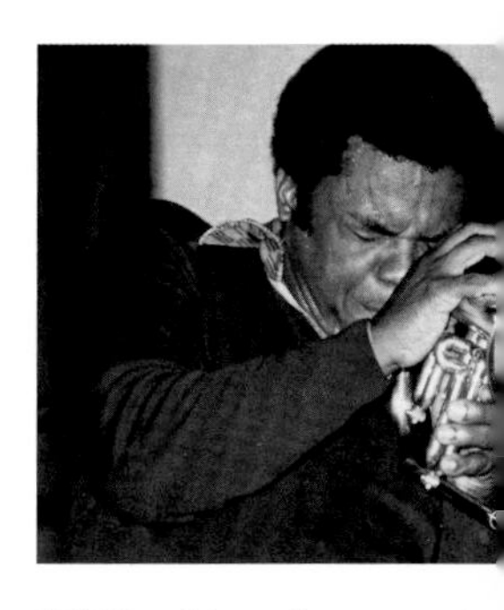

1970s Many famous rock bands and artists play in the original Fieldhouse.

The presidential medallion features academic symbols: owl (wisdom), laurel wreath (truth), scarab beetle (tenacity), lamp (knowledge).

1963 Classes begin with 226 students.

1963 James H. Zumberge serves as first president.

1967 Students participate in the first commencement ceremonies.

1960s ▶ 1970s

An early Grand Valley logo.

1965 Freshman students wear beanie caps, a custom imposed by the pioneer class.

1966 Copeland Living Center opens, first residential housing on the Allendale Campus.

1969 Arend D. Lubbers serves as second president.

THE FIRST 50 YEARS

PLANT
LIFE

1997 Grand Valley breaks ground for the Meijer Campus in Holland, continuing its community outreach efforts.

2000 Richard M. DeVos Center opens in Grand Rapids, with its distinctive Beckering Family Carillon tower.

2002 Football wins the first of four national championships. Women's soccer, basketball and volleyball would later win national crowns.

2006 Thomas J. Haas serves as the university's fourth president.

2003 Cook-DeVos Center for Health Sciences opens on Grand Rapids' "Medical Mile," housing nursing and health professions programs.

2000s

1998 Grand Valley hosts Science Olympiad National Tournament.

2001 New President Mark A. Murray addresses an impromptu crowd on September 11; he asks campus community members to show support and compassion for each other.

2003 MAREC serves as a self-sustaining distributive energy center; the move strengthens Grand Valley's commitment to sustainability. Later MAREC assists in building a manure-to-electricity plant at a dairy farm.

2008 Grand Valley launches first comprehensive campaign, Shaping Our Future, with first priority to raise funds for new library.

1988 L.V. Eberhard Center opens in downtown Grand Rapids.

1993 Grand Valley hosts Shakespeare Festival; event grows to Michigan's oldest and largest celebration of the Bard's works.

1994 The Meadows Golf Course opens. It has since hosted six NCAA national golf championships.

1996 Annis Water Resources Institute launches a second research vessel, the *W.G. Jackson*.

1990s

1987 Grand Valley receives university status from Michigan lawmakers.

1989 Enrollment climbs to more than 10,000 for the first time.

1995 Henry Hall, Padnos Hall of Science and Student Services Building open.

KIRKHOF CENTER
STUDENT SE

50 FAVORITE PIECES OF ARTWORK CREDITS

2 Place Lamartine **(page 83)**
Artist: Terence La Noue, American
Dated: 1984
Media: Mixed media on canvas
Dimension: 71 inches x 74 inches
Gift of the Richard and Roberta Lieberman Estate

A Brief Medical Encyclopedia **(page 83)**
Artist: Alexander Florensky, Russian
Dated: 2002
Media: Glazed ceramic tiles
Dimension: 15 1/2 feet x 12 1/2 feet
GVSU Commission

Actuality #8 **(page 83)**
Artist: Renee Zettle-Sterling, American
Dated: 2002
Media: Bronze, silver and copper
Dimension: 8 inches x 3.5 inches x 3.5 inches
Gift of the artist

Air Show **(page 84)**
Artist: Lisa Orr, American
Dated: 2002
Media: Stained glass, steel, iron
Dimension: ranges from 2 feet x 2 feet to 3 feet x 3 feet
GVSU Collection

Amaranth **(page 140)**
Artist: Cyril Lixenberg, Dutch
Dated: 2002
Media: Steel
Dimension: 15 feet x 5 feet x 5 feet
GVSU Commission

Arch **(page 84)**
Artist: Dmitry Kaminker, Russian
Dated: 1999
Media: Cast bronze
Dimension: 4 inches x 8.5 inches x 4 inches
GVSU Commission

Both Sides of the Brain Puzzlehead Series: A Visual Tribute to Physician Family Members **(page 84)**
Artist: Dewey Blocksma, American
Dated: 2003
Media: Mixed media, found objects
Dimension: 12 inches x 20 inches x 20 inches
GVSU Collection

Burger and Fries **(page 84)**
Artist: Angela Samuels, American
Dated: 2003
Media: Acrylic on canvas
Dimension: 12 inches x 12 inches x 2 inches
GVSU Commission

Clearing II **(page 84)**
Artist: David Shapiro, American
Dated: 1988
Media: Lithograph, embossed
Dimension: 24 inches x 56 inches
Gift of Ann and David Keister

Cone **(page 84)**
Artist: Eunmee Lee, Korean
Dated: 2008
Media: Ceramic
Dimension: 13 inches x 14 inches x 14.5 inches
GVSU Collection

The Embrace **(page 84)**
Artist: Joseph Kinnebrew, American
Dated: 2000
Media: Bronze
Dimension: 5 feet x 7 feet x 5 feet
GVSU Commission

Exporting of Knowledge **(page 152)**
Artist: Hubert Massey, American
Dated: 2000
Media: Fresco
Dimension: 5 feet x 7 feet
GVSU Commission

First Generation Artifact: Tatted Lace Collar **(page 84)**
Artist: Norwood Viviano, American
Dated: 2003
Media: Cast bronze
Dimension: 23 inches x 23 inches x 3/8 inches
GVSU Commission

Formation **(page 84)**
Artist: Daleene Menning, American
Dated: 1996
Media: Ceramic
Dimension: 48 feet x 6 feet (approx.)
GVSU Commission

Fortunes of Nature **(page 85)**
Artist: Harold Linton, American
Dated: 2000
Media: Acrylic on canvas and bent hardwoods: walnut, oaks, poplar, cherry
Dimension: 17 feet x 10 feet x 8 inches
GVSU Commission

Four Men Going Fishing, 6a District, Ghana **(page 85)**
Artist: Dan Watts, American
Dated: 2007
Media: Photograph
Dimension: 16 inches x 22 inches
GVSU Collection

France Champagne **(page 85)**
Artist: Pierre Bonnard, French
Dated: 1891
Media: Color lithographic poster
Dimension: 32.75 inches x 24.5 inches
The Robert L. Hoskins and Erwin A. Raible Collection of Fin de Siècle French Prints, gift of Elaine Rutowski Shay

Function or Submarine **(page 85)**
Artist: Hoon Lee, Korean
Dated: 2008
Media: Bamboo
Dimension: 40 inches x 144 inches
GVSU Collection

Great Sand Dunes National Monument, Colorado **(page 85)**
Artist: David Lubbers, American
Dated: 1983
Media: Photograph
Dimension: 19 inches x 15 inches
Gift of Ray and Carol Stevens

GVSU Marching Band **(page 85)**
Artist: Stuart Padnos, American
Dated: 1998
Media: Mixed media, metal
Dimension: 40 feet x 7 feet x 7 feet
Gift of Stuart Padnos, in memory of his wife

I Will/I Must **(page 85)**
Artist: Jeff Colby, American
Dated: 1995
Media: Collage
Dimension: 4 inches x 6 inches
Gift of the Colby Foundation

I'm Halfway There... **(page 85)**
Artist: Jason McChristian, American
Dated: 2006
Media: Oil on panel
Dimension: 72 inches x 96 inches
Gift of Jason McChristian

In Reverence of Remedies **(page 42)**
Artist: Julie Upmeyer, American
Dated: 2002
Media: Mixed media
Dimension: 120 inches x 420 inches
GVSU Commission

Indian Musician Playing Tabla **(page 85)**
Artist: Indian Folk Artist, Indian
Dated: Not Dated
Media: Hand-carved wood
Dimension: 36 inches x 14.5 inches x 15 inches
GVSU Collection

La Catrina y Calavera del Siglo XX **(page 86)**
Artist: Jose Guadalupe Posada, Mexican
Dated: 2004
Media: Restrike print
Dimension: 8.5 inches x 11 inches
GVSU Collection

Levels of Knowledge **(page 86)**
Artist: Ed Wong-Ligda, American
Dated: 2005
Media: Oil on canvas
Dimension: 72 inches x 108 inches
GVSU Commission

Little Red **(page 86)**
Artist: John Phillips, American
Dated: 2007
Media: Acrylic on canvas
Dimension: 50 inches x 40 inches
GVSU Collection

Luminosity #1, #142, #149 **(page 86)**
Artist: David Huang, American
Dated: 2000
Media: Bronze, sterling silver, 23-karat gold leaf
Dimension: 3 inches x 3 inches to 7.5 inches x 5 inches
GVSU Collection

Magna Matter **(page 86)**
Artist: Elona Van Gent, American
Dated: 2004
Media: Rapid prototyping sculpture
Dimension: 11 inches x 23 inches x 15 inches
GVSU Collection

Memory **(page 86)**
Artist: Ann Keister, American
Dated: 1998
Media: Wool tapestry
Dimension: 68 inches x 116 inches
GVSU Commission

The Mouse Trap **(page 64)**
Artist: Andy Twietmeyer, American
Dated: 1995
Media: Oil on canvas
Dimension: 50 inches x 60 inches
GVSU Commission

Mundus Imaginalis: Corpus Cognoscendi (Body of Knowledge) **(page 86)**
Artist: Paul Wittenbraker, American
Dated: 2000
Media: Documentation photograph (configuration)
Dimension: 20 inches x 31 inches
GVSU Commission

No Why (Suite) **(page 86)**
Artist: Dellas Henke, American
Dated: 2004
Media: Engraving and aquatint paint
Dimension: 7 inches x 6 inches
GVSU Collection

Paleolithic Red **(page 86)**
Artist: Sam Gilliam, American
Dated: 1993
Media: Acrylic on polypropylene
Dimension: 37 inches x 81 inches
Gift of William and Glenda Noakes

Pansies **(page 87)**
Artist: Jo Hormuth, American
Dated: 1999-2003
Media: Wool, felt and resin
Dimension: range from 12 inches x 12 inches to 36 inches x 36 inches
GVSU Collection

Polychrome Acoma Vessel **(page 87)**
Artist: Robert Patricio, Native American
Dated: ca. 2008
Media: Polychrome ceramic
Dimension: 9 inches x 10 inches
GVSU Collection

Reflection of a Hunter Goddess **(page 87)**
Artist: Tim Fisher, American
Dated: 1998
Media: Oil on wood
Dimension: 48 inches x 80 inches
GVSU Collection

Siphonophores **(page 87)**
Artist: Beverly Seley, American
Dated: 2000
Media: Copper, bronze, sterling silver and brass
Dimension: 24 inches x 7 inches x 7 inches
GVSU Collection

Studying Drips **(page 87)**
Artist: Adam Tetzlaff, American
Dated: ca. 2005
Media: Acrylic on Canvas
Dimension: 21.5 inches x 21.5 inches
GVSU Collection

Tablet **(page 87)**
Artist: Herb Babcock, American
Dated: Not dated
Media: Cast glass, steel
Dimension: 14 inches x 20 inches x 3 inches
GVSU Commission

Tall Feats and Long Strides **(page 87)**
Artist: Carrie Wilson, American
Dated: 2005
Media: Fabric, steel, aluminum and styrofoam
Dimension: 4.5 inches x 129 inches x 14 inches
GVSU Commission

Tao (The Way) **(page 87)**
Artist: Peimin Ni, Chinese
Dated: 1996
Media: Ink on handmade paper
Dimension: 22 inches x 26 inches
Gift of the artist

Transformational Link **(page 81)**
Artist: Gary Kulak, American
Dated: 1990
Media: Painted steel
Dimension: 40 feet x 47 feet x 20 feet
GVSU Collection

Untitled **(page 87)**
Artist: Stephen Duren, American
Dated: ca. 1990
Media: Oil on canvas
Dimension: 12 feet x 9 feet
Anonymous gift given in honor of Stephen Duren

Untitled **(page 88)**
Artist: Jill Eggers, American
Dated: 1999
Media: Oil on canvas
Dimension: 54 inches x 64 inches
GVSU Commission

Untitled **(page 88)**
Artist: Mark Ripley, American
Dated: 1987
Media: Gouche, graphite, ink on paper
Dimension: 44 inches x 60 inches
Gift of William Lieberman, in honor of Paris Tennenhouse

Village Harmony **(page 88)**
Artist: Hao Bo Yi, Chinese
Dated: 1983
Media: Woodcut
Dimension: 27.25 inches x 18.25 inches
GVSU Collection

Which for Whom? **(page 88)**
Artist: Steven Sorman, American
Dated: 2005
Media: Print
Dimension: 22 inches x 30 inches
GVSU Collection

Workers in a Field (the Conversation) **(page 88)**
Artist: Mathias Alten, German-born American
Dated: 1916
Media: Oil on canvas
Dimension: 26 inches x 32 inches
Gift of George H. and Barbara Gordon

Zonder Titel (Untitled) **(page 88)**
Artist: Karel Appel, Dutch
Artist: Peirre Alechinsky, Belgian
Dated: 1978
Media: Lithograph
Dimension: 8.5 inches x 11.75 inches
The Cyril Lixenberg Collection of Contemporary Dutch Prints, a gift of the Brooks Family

INDEXES

BOARD OF TRUSTEES MEMBERS

EXECUTIVE OFFICERS

The university has changed the titles of executive officers over the years. This list indicates years of service for members of the senior management team and their final title at Grand Valley.

Philip W. Buchen	Vice President for Business Affairs	1963-1966
David H. Jones	Vice President for Business and Finance	1967-1971
Kenneth R. Venderbush	Vice President for Student Affairs	1970-1973
Roy S. Lumsden	Vice President for College Relations	1971-1974
Arthur C. Hills	Executive Assistant to the President; Secretary, Board of Trustees	1971-1988
Harold M. Kolenbrander	Assistant to the President	1972-1973
Bruce A. Loessin	Vice President for Institutional Development	1973-1981
Glenn A. Niemeyer	Provost and Vice President for Academic Affairs	1973-2001
Ronald F. VanSteeland	Vice President for Finance and Administration; Treasurer, Board of Trustees	1973-2001
Matthew E. McLogan	Vice President for University Relations	1987-
Thomas A. Butcher	University Counsel	1989-
Jean W. Enright	Executive Assistant to the President; Secretary, Board of Trustees	1988-2004
Maribeth Wardrop	Vice President for Development	2000-
John A. Gracki	Interim Provost and Vice President for Academic Affairs	2001-2002
Timothy O. Schad	Vice President for Finance and Administration; Treasurer, Board of Trustees	2001-2007
Gayle R. Davis	Provost and Vice President for Academic Affairs	2002-
Patricia Oldt	Vice President for Planning and Equity	2002-2008
Teri L. Losey	Special Assistant to the President; Secretary, Board of Trustees	2005-
James D. Bachmeier	Vice President for Finance and Administration; Treasurer, Board of Trustees	2007-
Jeanne J. Arnold	Vice President for Inclusion and Equity	2008-

DEANS OF COLLEGES

This list includes deans of faculty in academic units (called "colleges" or "divisions" at various times during the history of Grand Valley).

George Potter	Dean of Faculty	1967-1970
Glenn A. Niemeyer	Dean, College of Arts and Sciences	1970-1973
T. Dan Gilmore	Dean, Thomas Jefferson College	1970-1976
Kenneth Venderbush	Acting Dean, William James College	1971-1972
Robert J. Toft	Dean, College IV	1972-1975
Adrian Tinsley	Dean, William James College	1972-1980
John Linnell	Dean, College of Arts and Sciences	1973-1975
Marvin G. DeVries	Dean, F.E. Seidman Graduate College of Business	1973-1979
Carl Arendsen	Acting Dean, College IV	1975-1976
John A. Gracki	Acting Dean, College of Arts and Sciences	1975-1976
John A. Gracki	Dean, College of Arts and Sciences	1976-1979
P. Douglas Kindschi	Dean, College IV	1976-1979
Phyllis T. Thompson	Dean, Thomas Jefferson College	1977-1980
Marvin G. DeVries	Dean, F.E. Seidman College of Business and Administration	1979-1983
P. Douglas Kindschi	Dean, Kirkhof College	1979-1983
Charles W. Sorensen	Dean, College of Arts and Sciences	1979-1983
Forrest Armstrong	Dean, William James College	1980-1983
Charles W. Sorensen	Dean, Social Sciences	1983-1984
Marvin G. DeVries	Dean, Seidman School of Business	1983-1988
Forrest Armstrong	Dean, Arts and Humanities	1983-1997
P. Douglas Kindschi	Dean, Science and Mathematics	1983-2004
Anthony Travis	Dean, Social Sciences	1984-1994
Eugene Klippel	Acting Dean, Seidman School of Business	1988-1989
Stanton Lindquist	Acting Dean, Seidman School of Business	1989-1990; 1998-1999
Glenn Pitman	Dean, Seidman School of Business	1990-1994

Irving Berkowitz	Dean, School of Social Work	1993-1994
Allan Ten Eyck	Dean, School of Education	1993-1996
Mary Horan	Dean, Kirkhof School of Nursing	1993-1997
Emery Turner	Dean, Seidman School of Business	1994-1998
Nancy Harper	Dean, Social Sciences	1994-1999
Rodney Mulder	Dean, School of Social Work	1994-2004
Robert Hagerty	Dean, School of Education	1996-2001
David McGee	Acting Dean, Arts and Humanities	1997-1998
Lorraine Rodrigues-Fisher	Dean, Kirkhof School of Nursing	1997-2000
Gary Stark	Dean, Arts and Humanities	1998-2001
Jonathan White	Dean, Social Sciences	1999-2002
David Mielke	Dean, Seidman School of Business	1999-2003
Phyllis Gendler	Dean, Kirkhof College of Nursing	2000-2007
Anne Mulder	Interim Dean, School of Education	2001-2003
Jon Jellema	Dean, Arts and Humanities	2001-2004
Erika King	Dean, Social Sciences	2002-2004
John Reifel	Interim Dean, Seidman School of Business	2003-2004
Elaine Collins	Dean, College of Education	2003-
Robert Beasecker	Interim Dean, University Libraries	2004-2005
Rodney Mulder	Dean, College of Community and Public Service	2004-2008
Jane Toot	Dean, College of Health Professions	2004-2008
Frederick Antczak	Dean, College of Liberal Arts and Sciences	2004-
Paul Plotkowski	Dean, Padnos College of Engineering and Computing	2004-
Wendy Wenner	Dean, Brooks College of Interdisciplinary Studies	2004-
H. James Williams	Dean, Seidman College of Business	2004-
Lee VanOrsdel	Dean, University Libraries	2005-
Cynthia McCurren	Dean, Kirkhof College of Nursing	2007-
George Grant, Jr.	Dean, College of Community and Public Service	2008-
Roy H. Olsson, Jr.	Dean, College of Health Professions	2008-

NAMED BUILDINGS ON CAMPUS

CAMPUS BUILDING	NAMED FOR	COMPLETED	
Copeland Living Center	James M. Copeland	1966	Member, Board of Trustees
Robinson Living Center	Kenneth W. Robinson	1967	Member, Board of Trustees
Zumberge Library	James H. Zumberge	1969	President, 1962-1968
Kistler Living Center	Grace Olsen Kistler	1971	Member, Board of Trustees
Kirkhof Center	Russel H. Kirkhof	1973	Entrepreneur, Inventor
Hoobler Living Center	Icie Macy Hoobler	1987	Member, Board of Trustees
Johnson Living Center	Paul A. Johnson	1987	Member, Board of Trustees
Ott Living Center	Arnold C. Ott	1987	Member, Board of Trustees
Weed Living Center	Ella Koeze Weed	1987	Member, Board of Trustees
Eberhard Center	L.V. Eberhard	1988	Founder, Eberhard's, grocery chain
DeVos Living Center	Richard M. DeVos	1989	Co-founder of Amway; Member, Board of Trustees
Kleiner Commons	A. Robert Kleiner	1989	Member, Board of Trustees
Pew Living Center	Robert C. Pew	1989	Member, Board of Trustees
Pickard Living Center	William F. Pickard	1989	Member, Board of Trustees
Cook-DeWitt Center	Peter and Pat Cook Marvin and Jerene DeWitt	1991	Owner, Mazda Great Lakes Co-founder, Bil-Mar Foods
Cook Carillon Tower	Peter and Pat Cook	1994	Owner, Mazda Great Lakes
Henry Hall	Paul B. Henry	1995	Former U.S. Representative
Padnos Hall of Science	Seymour and Esther Padnos	1995	Co-manager, Louis Padnos Iron & Metal Company
Calder Art Center	Alexander Calder	1997	Acclaimed American sculptor
Swanson Living Center	Maxine M. Swanson	1997	Member, Board of Trustees
Seidman Living Center	L. William and Sally Seidman	1997	Founder of Grand Valley
Kirkpatrick Living Center	William F. Kirkpatrick	1998	Member, Board of Trustees
Stafford Living Center	Dale Stafford	1998	Member, Board of Trustees

CAMPUS BUILDING	NAMED FOR	COMPLETED	
Richard M. DeVos Center	Richard M. DeVos	2000	Co-founder of Amway; Member, Board of Trustees
Keller Engineering Building	Fred M. Keller	2000	Owner, Paragon Tool and Die
Secchia Hall	Peter F. Secchia	2000	Former U.S. Ambassador to Italy
Frey Living Center	Edward J. Frey	2001	Banking, Insurance Leader; Member, Board of Trustees
Hills Living Center	Arthur C. Hills	2001	Secretary, Board of Trustees; Composer, Grand Valley Alma Mater
Cook-DeVos Center for Health Sciences	Peter and Pat Cook Richard M. DeVos	2003	Owner, Mazda Great Lakes Co-founder of Amway; Member, Board of Trustees
Murray Living Center	Mark A. Murray	2004	President, 2001-2006
VanSteeland Living Center	Ronald F. VanSteeland	2004	Executive Officer, retired 2001
Kennedy Hall of Engineering	John C. Kennedy	2007	President, Autocam Corporation; Member, Board of Trustees
Honors College	Frederik Meijer	2008	Chairman Emeritus, Meijer Inc.
Niemeyer Learning and Living Center	Glenn A. Niemeyer	2008	Provost, retired 2001

PHOTO CREDITS

All photos courtesy of University Archives, except as indicated below:

FOREWORDS BY THREE PRESIDENTS

page i: photo by Bernadine Carey-Tucker

A STORY BUILT ONE BRICK AT A TIME

page 1, 3: photos courtesy of Grand Rapids History & Special Collections, Archive, Grand Rapids Public Library, Grand Rapids, Michigan

page 4: (top) photo courtesy of Grand Rapids History & Special Collections, Archive, Grand Rapids Public Library, Grand Rapids, Michigan

LEADERS

page 7: (top left, center left and bottom right) photos by Amanda Pitts (top right) photo by Frederic A. Reinecke (bottom center) photo by Bernadine Carey-Tucker

page 16: (top) News and Information Services archives (bottom) photo by Amanda Pitts

page 18: (bottom) photo by Bernadine Carey-Tucker

page 19: photo by Adam Bird

page 20: photos by Bernadine Carey-Tucker

page 21: (top) photo by Frederic A. Reinecke (bottom) photo by Bernadine Carey-Tucker

page 22: (top) photo by Adam Bird (bottom) photo by Bernadine Carey-Tucker

page 23: photos by Bernadine Carey-Tucker

page 24: photos by Bernadine Carey-Tucker

page 25: photo by Courtney Newbauer

page 26: photos by Bernadine Carey-Tucker

page 27: photos by Bernadine Carey-Tucker

page 28: photo by Bernadine Carey-Tucker

page 29: (top left) photo by Amanda Pitts (top right and bottom) photos by Bernadine Carey-Tucker

page 30: (top) photo by Amanda Pitts (bottom left) photo courtesy of Facilities Planning (bottom right) photo by Dianne Carroll Burdick

page 31: photo by Bernadine Carey-Tucker

page 32: (left) photo by Bernadine Carey-Tucker (right) photo by Amanda Pitts

ACADEMIC MILESTONES

page 33 (top center and bottom left) photos courtesy of Barbara H. Padnos International Center (center right) photo by Andrew Terzes

page 41: News and Information Services archives

page 42: photo by Bernadine Carey-Tucker

page 43: (left) photo by Bernadine Carey-Tucker (right) photo courtesy of Barbara H. Padnos International Center

page 44: (top) photo by Bernadine Carey-Tucker (bottom) News and Information Services archives

page 45: (bottom) photo by Amanda Pitts

page 46: (left) photo by Amanda Pitts (right) photo by Bernadine Carey-Tucker

page 47: (left) photo by Bernadine Carey-Tucker (right) photo courtesy of Hauenstein Center for Presidential Studies

page 48: (left) photo by Amanda Pitts (right) photo courtesy of WMSTI

STUDENT LIFE

page 49: (top right) News and Information Services archives

page 63: photo courtesy of Cassonya Carter-Pugh

page 64: (top left) photo by Bernadine Carey-Tucker (top right) photo by Amanda Pitts (bottom left) photo by Brianne Goodyear (bottom right) photo by Bernadine Carey-Tucker

page 65: (top) News and Information Services archives (bottom) photo by Bernadine Carey-Tucker

page 66: photo by Bernadine Carey-Tucker

ARTS AND CULTURE

page 67: (top center and bottom center) photos courtesy of Theatre at Grand Valley (center left) photo by Bernadine Carey-Tucker (bottom left) photo courtesy of WGVU (bottom right) photo by Brianne Goodyear

page 71: (bottom right) photo courtesy of the *Grand Rapids Press*

page 72: (bottom) photo by Bernadine Carey-Tucker

page 73: (top) photo by Bernadine Carey-Tucker (bottom) photo courtesy of Music Department

page 74: (left) photo by Bernadine Carey-Tucker (center) photo by Phil Schaafsma (right) photo by Amanda Pitts

page 75: photos courtesy of Theatre at Grand Valley

page 76: photo courtesy of Grand Rapids History & Special Collections, Archive, Grand Rapids Public Library, Grand Rapids, Michigan

pages 77-78: photos courtesy of Theatre at Grand Valley (poster on page 77 by Bob Bauer)

page 79: (bottom) photo by Adam Bird

page 80: photo by Jan Lewis

page 81: (top) photo by Adam Bird

page 82: photos by Amanda Pitts

page 89: photo by Dianne Carroll Burdick, courtesy of the *Advance Newspapers*

page 90: (top) photo by Amanda Pitts (bottom) News and Information Services archives

page 91: photo courtesy of the GVSU Art Gallery

page 92: photo by Bernadine Carey-Tucker

page 93: (top) photo by Frederic A. Reinecke (bottom left) News and Information Services archives (bottom right) photo by Amanda Pitts

page 94: (right) photo by Bernadine Carey-Tucker

page 95: photo by Dianne Carroll Burdick

page 96: (right) photo by Bernadine Carey-Tucker

pages 97-101: photos courtesy of WGVU

page 102: photo by Amanda Pitts

ATHLETICS

page 103: all photos courtesy of Sports Information, except (center row) courtesy of University Archives and (bottom right) by Amanda Pitts

pages 105-120: all photos courtesy of Sports Information, except as noted

page 110: (bottom) News and Information Services archives

page 112: (bottom) photo by Bernadine Carey-Tucker

page 1114: (bottom right) photo by Bernadine Carey-Tucker

page 119: (bottom) photo by Steve King/KingStudios

CAMPUS GROWTH

page 121: (top left) photo by Amanda Pitts (top right) photo by Bernadine Carey-Tucker (bottom right) photo by Amanda Pitts

page 130: (right) photo by Amanda Pitts

page 131: (top) News and Information Services archives

page 133: (bottom) photo by Bernadine Carey-Tucker

page 134: News and Information Services archives

page 136: photos by Bernadine Carey-Tucker

page 137: photos by Bernadine Carey-Tucker

page 138: photo by Adam Bird

page 139: (top) photo by Amanda Pitts (bottom) News and Information Services archives

page 140: (top) photo by Courtney Newbauer (bottom) photo by Bernadine Carey-Tucker

SUCCESS STORIES

page 141: photo by Phil Schaafsma

page 143: photo by Amanda Pitts

page 144: (top) photo by Carl Sanford (bottom) photo by Michael Tobias

page 145: photo by Amanda Pitts

page 146: photo by Stephanie Berger

page 147: photo by Amanda Pitts

page 148: photo by Amanda Pitts

page 149: photo by Amanda Pitts

page 150: photo by Andrew Terzes

page 151: photo by Amanda Pitts

page 152: photos by Bernadine Carey-Tucker

page 153: photo by Amanda Pitts

page 154: photo by Amanda Pitts

page 155: photo by Bernadine Carey-Tucker

page 156: photo by Amanda Pitts

page 157: photo by Amanda Pitts

TIMELINE

(opening photos of ravines) photos by Amanda Pitts (Allendale Campus) photo by Andrew Terzes

ACKNOWLEDGMENTS

Grand Valley Celebrates 50 Years of Shaping Lives

PROJECT STAFF

Teri Losey – 50th Anniversary Committee chair

Mary Eilleen Lyon – executive editor and writer

Michele Coffill – editor and writer

Dottie Barnes, Brian J. Bowe, Mary Isca Pirkola – contributing editors and writers

Bernadine Carey-Tucker – photography services manager and contributing photographer

Amanda Pitts – photographer

Elizabeth Lienau – photography coordinator

Sherry Bouwman – editorial assistant

Rhonda Lubberts – executive creative director

Nancy J. Crittenden – project and marketing manager

Jacqueline Cuppy – creative director

John Zerfas – designer

Kyle Douglass – distribution

Dave Poortvliet, Ben Rapin and Kelley Rogers – online support

SPECIAL THANKS TO:

Grand Valley Board of Trustees: Sue C. Carnell; Dorothy A. Johnson; Noreen K. Myers, vice chair; Shelley E. Padnos; Lucille S. Taylor; Michael D. Thomas; David L. Way; Kate Pew Wolters, chair; Thomas J. Haas, ex officio

Matthew E. McLogan, vice president for University Relations

Chris Barbee, alumni relations director

Robert Beasecker, director university archives

Henry Matthews, director of galleries and collections

Robbi Osipoff, 50th anniversary project coordinator

Nancy Richard, university archivist